THE SLOW BURNING LOVE OF GOD

HAROLD KLEMP

MAHANTA TRANSCRIPTS

BOOK 13

ECKANKAR
Minneapolis

The Slow Burning Love of God, Mahanta Transcripts, Book 13

Copyright © 1996, 1997 ECKANKAR

Printed in U.S.A.

Compiled by Mary Carroll Moore
Edited by Joan Klemp and Anthony Moore

Text Illustrations by April Munson
Text photo (page xii) by Bernard Chouet
Back cover photo by Robert Huntley

Second Edition — 1997

Library of Congress Cataloging-in-Publication Data

Klemp, Harold.
    The slow burning love of God / Harold Klemp.
        p. cm. — (Mahanta transcripts ; bk. 13)
    Includes index.
    ISBN 1-57043-130-2
    1. Eckankar (Organization) — Doctrines. 2. Spiritual life —
Eckankar (Organization) I. Title. II. Series: Klemp, Harold.
Mahanta transcripts ; bk. 13.
[BP605.E3K567 1997]
299'.93 — dc21   97-8007
                                                     CIP

♾ The paper used in this publication meets the minimum requirements of the American National Standard for Information Sciences — Permanence of Paper for Printed Library Materials, ANSI Z39.48-1984.

CONTENTS

• Listening to God • Hearts Full of Love • Hanging Curtains • River of Life • Talk Planning • A Very Spiritual Journey • *The Flute of God* • At the Post Office • Worth More than a Dollar • Crimes against Soul • Help in Your Search for God

FOREWORD

The teachings of ECK define the nature of Soul. You are Soul, a particle of God sent into the worlds (including earth) to gain spiritual experience.

The goal in ECK is spiritual freedom in this lifetime, after which you become a Co-worker with God, both here and in the next world. Karma and reincarnation are primary beliefs.

Key to the ECK teachings is the Mahanta, the Living ECK Master. He has the special ability to act as both the Inner and Outer Master for ECK students. He is the prophet of Eckankar, given respect but not worship. He teaches the sacred name of God, HU, which lifts you spiritually into the Light and Sound of God, the ECK (Holy Spirit). Purified by the practice of the Spiritual Exercises of ECK, you are then able to accept the full love of God in this lifetime.

Sri Harold Klemp is the Mahanta, the Living ECK Master. He has written many books, discourses, and articles about the spiritual life. Many of his public talks are available on audio- and video-cassette. His teachings uplift people and help them recognize and understand their own experiences in the Light and Sound of God.

The Slow Burning Love of God, Mahanta Transcripts, Book 13, contains his talks from 1993 to 1994. May they help you find love, wisdom, and spiritual freedom.

Sri Harold Klemp, the Mahanta, the Living ECK Master tells how to live a spiritually fulfilling life: "If you would have love, you must first give love. And if you give divine love to others, you shall have divine love for yourself."

1

GIVING — THE
SECRET TO GETTING

On the plane a few days ago, I sat next to a gentleman who lives in the Midwest. He was flying to California to take care of his mother and his half sister. Both are in their eighties.

The man does this every month. He stops first in Los Angeles and takes care of his half sister for a while. After three or four days, he gets on a plane and flies to San Jose where his mother lives. He takes care of her for a while, then he flies back to his home in the Midwest. Then he does it all over again the next month.

It's an interesting thing. This man told me he was sixty, but he looks a full ten years younger.

GIVING TO OTHERS

He said his half sister is losing her memory.

She lives in a trailer park for senior citizens. Each time he flies in to see her, he asks her to come get him at the airport. One time she didn't come, so the man called her at home. "Remember," he said, "I spoke to you yesterday and said I was coming in today. You were going to pick me up at the airport."

"But today is bridge club," she said.

"Yes, but you said you were going to come get me," he reminded her.

"Today is bridge club," she said again.

Other times, when she does make it to the airport to get him, she forgets where she parks the car.

"What do you do when that happens?" I asked him.

"I station her up in the observation deck. Then I jog back and forth up and down the rows of cars in the parking lot. I spend a lot of time jogging," he added.

"It must be very hard on you," I said.

"No," he answered, "a little jog around the parking lot isn't that much. It just takes a long time." He told me he likes to run marathons. He travels all around the world to do this. So I understood why an airport parking lot isn't that big to him.

We make our own problems, then later we complain about them.

He wasn't complaining about his half sister forgetting where she parked the car. But I was thinking later that it made a funny story. He is very much the way most of us are. We make our own problems, then later we complain about them.

You'd think if his half sister forgot to pick him up at the airport a few times or if he had to run through the rain a few times looking for the car, he'd catch on. Well, he finally did. For the first time last month, he asked a friend of hers at the trailer park to come along. This gentleman loves to watch the airplanes, and with two of them coming to the airport, they always remember where she parks the car.

This is his solution. It saves him a great deal of time.

THANKS

Although he takes care of his half sister, all he gets for thanks from her is her cane. She is very quick with it. They often have words. This man looks very relaxed but he has his temper too.And his half sister, although she is in her eighties, is quite a strong woman. "The family genes have this extraordinary strength," the man told me.

One time she said she would like to go on a cruise with him and his wife. He has his own business and can take care of many of these financial needs. So he took her on a cruise to the Caribbean for a week.

While they were on the cruise ship, there was a man who put on a gorilla costume to entertain the guests and liven things up a little. When the gorilla man approached the half sister, she let him have it with her cane. "I think he was surprised," the man said.

The man brought his half sister back home after giving her this nice trip; a month later he asked her how she'd enjoyed it.

"How'd you like the cruise?" he asked her. "What cruise?" she said.

"I spent a lot of money on planes and boats," he answered. "And I'm sure the gorilla man will never forget you."

"What gorilla man?" she said. She didn't remember a thing, even when he showed her the photographs he'd taken of the trip.

"All that money," he told me, "and she doesn't remember a thing." I was laughing by this time. "It makes you think, doesn't it?" I said. He's a businessman, and I could see he watches the dollar very carefully. "Yeah, when I think of all that money, and she doesn't remember a thing," he said.

But he seems to get something out of the relationship. He likes his half sister. He enjoys taking her out to a restaurant when they are together; they laugh and fight, but they enjoy each other. And as soon as he leaves, she forgets the whole weekend.

This is an example of a person who is giving of himself to others.

On the surface it appears that he gets nothing out of it for himself. But he is developing a great deal of patience. "Doesn't it get hard sometimes?" I asked. "Somebody's got to do it," he told me. "When you get to be my age, you run into it more and more. Those of us who can, we do. We just do it because we do it."

In his own way he was expressing a deep love, divine love. He didn't have to do it; he didn't have to put up with the cane. But he enjoyed the people he was with, his family and their friends. He was giving of himself and opening his heart.

Facing life gracefully is probably the first step to giving of yourself to others.

COMPLEMENTARY QUALITIES

We've just come from the spiritual Year of Graceful Living into the spiritual Year of Giving. As if you can stop doing one, as if you can stop being graceful as you go into the Year of Giving. I don't know if that's possible.

Facing life gracefully is probably the first step to giving of yourself to others.

They aren't separate qualities. The quality of being graceful in your dealings with other people or in giving of yourself to life go together. They complement each other.

When I first mentioned the Year of Giving, some people were upset. "Sounds too much like money," they said. And I was thinking there are so many hundreds of ways to give of yourself without opening your wallet. People assume that as soon as you're in a religion or a church, someone's going to grab you by the elbow and say, "OK, give." Donations are important, that's true. But unless you have learned to open your heart to life—to other people, to God— your gifts of deed or money count for very little.

The Year of Giving means a year of learning how to open your heart and let the ECK, Divine Spirit, help you become a greater and better person.

WHAT IS OUR PURPOSE?

I've mentioned so often that our purpose here is to become a Co-worker with God.

Knowing that this is our goal gives meaning to the experiences we encounter in life. Why are people surly? Why are we grouchy? Well, we're working things out with ourselves and with our neighbors, with our families and our loved ones. Because we're trying to reach not physical but spiritual perfection.

We know too well that the human body wears down. It runs down very much like a clock, one of the old windup clocks. It just runs down. You can wind it up, and the minutes go on ticking by for so many hours. But after a while it runs down, and you have to wind it up again. This is the human side of life. We're not looking for perfection or life everlasting in a physical sense; we're looking to become more spiritual.

What we're trying to do is open our hearts to divine love, so we can become instruments of God, so we can start serving God.

INSTRUMENTS OF GOD

Most of us say, "I don't like the word *serving*." People who have no interest in growing spiritually—

What we're trying to do is open our hearts to divine love, so we can become instruments of God, so we can start serving God.

I mean truly growing spiritually—will have a reaction to serving others.

But the people who have served mankind best are the ones who have served mankind the most. Religious leaders, sometimes political leaders, economic leaders. People like Abraham Lincoln, Jesus, perhaps a scientist like Einstein. They put a whole new spin on creation and on reality, so that most people have no idea at all what they're talking about. But because they have manifested a certain idea, changes occur in the lives of many people.

FIGURING OUT A PROBLEM

During the past summer a group of ECKists were having a retreat at a YWCA camp up in Canada. They had a good time with the activities and meetings. But Saturday evening the camp director, who was not an ECKist, made an announcement.

"We've lost our fresh water supply," she said. There would be no showers that night.

A groan went up from everyone. They had been outdoors all day, and although camp is camp, it still feels good to have a shower. But there was no water. And the camp director didn't know what to do.

The Mahanta is the inner guide of the initiates in ECK.

One of the ECKists was a mechanical engineer. He went to the camp director and offered his help, and she was glad to accept it. She led him to the pump house and opened the door. The ECKist just looked at the maze of pipes inside and wondered where to begin. So he said to the Mahanta, *Let me see if I can work through this logically.*

The Mahanta is the inner guide of the initiates in ECK. It's the inner side of myself, the person who appears in dreams and teaches you there, who gives you the secret teachings of ECK. On the outer I give you what I can, but it's mostly to make a connection for those of you who are ready, willing, and able to go into the other worlds in your dreams, for those who want to know about truth, know about divine love, know about wisdom and many other things that are available for Soul to gain on Its path home to God. This knowledge is available. But many times people in ECK call upon the Mahanta for help or protection.

Many times people in ECK call upon the Mahanta for help or protection.

In this case, the ECKist needed help figuring out a problem. The camp wasn't getting any water, which was an inconvenience for a great number of people. Nothing serious, but — if you will pardon the expression — it was enough to dampen the weekend.

Reversing the Flow

The ECKist checked the pipes, did some tests, and found that the two water softeners in the pump house had plugged up. The backwash cycle wasn't working. A water softener has to go through a cycle to cleanse itself, it has to reverse the flow of water. Because this cleansing cycle wasn't happening in the two water softeners, the water flow to the showers had stopped. So the ECKist was able to fix the problem by bypassing the two water softeners. When he told the others that they could take showers now, everyone cheered.

Then one of them asked, "What was the problem?"

The ECKist explained that the flow had to be reversed. And since this was a meeting of ECK initiates, they all knew what he was talking about.

When people first come to the path of ECK or any other religion, they are so used to asking. They are used to begging God to fulfill their needs. Very few people ever think of giving something back to God, to life, or to others. The ECKists understood that when the engineer said the direction of the flow needed to be reversed, it was now time to give.

It was now time to give of themselves, their talents, and the divine love of the Holy Spirit that was flowing through them. It was time to give to others.

HOW TO LET GO

Sometimes there's not just a need to give to others but there's a need to give up something that's been holding you back in your own life. For example, we sometimes find that we become very attached to an idea, a person, a situation—or even a car.

An ECKist had driven a station wagon for almost eleven years. But it was getting old, and he knew that repairs were going to become more and more expensive. It was time to find a new car. Being a very careful and methodical person, this individual visited different car dealerships and test-drove eight or nine different cars.

He didn't care much about material things. He knew that the fewer things he had to clutter up his life, the more freedom he would have to do whatever he wanted to do, and being without a lot of belongings up to that time, he had had a lot of freedom. But now he needed to get a car, and if he needed to get one, he was going to do it right.

Finally the ECKist found a car. The price was right, but the car also had air conditioning and electric windows.

His other car, being eleven years old, was a stripped-down model, basically a steering wheel, four tires, and an engine. When he drove it, it was hard work—hard on the car, hard on the driver. When he got his new car, it was so easy and smooth. It liked to run. He reached the highway, and before he knew it he was driving over the speed limit. He'd have to watch the speedometer carefully when he drove this new car, he decided.

But his attitude began to change with his new car. This surprised him. He hadn't cared much about material things before, so he was surprised at his love for this new car. He really liked it. He liked it so much he even changed the radio stations he listened to in the car. He also promised himself to be very careful when he parked it so that someone wouldn't put a ding in it.

One day the ECKist went shopping at the supermarket after work. He looked for the right place to park his new car. He wanted to give the car every chance not to be hit.

There are rules about where to park in parking lots. Not on the end, so goes the wisdom, because one side of the car is always exposed. Never park next to a van because when you want to back up, you can't see. You might back into somebody who is coming along too fast. The ECKist followed all these little wisdoms.

That day all he could find was a parking spot where the right side of his car wasn't protected. But, he reasoned, if he went into the store, shopped fast, and came out really quickly, the car would be OK.

When I go into a store I take my time. I look here, I look there; my speed is very slow. I go down the aisles, reading all the labels on different things. When I get to the end of the aisle, I can't remember what the first labels said, so I have to go back and read them again. To my wife, a store's a store. She believes that if you're going to go in to buy something, you get it and go. She flies down the aisles, and things fly into the basket. While I wander around reading labels, she gets the food, then she comes and finds me. I'm usually in the same aisle where she left me. Unless I'm being stubborn; then I'll go into another area where she doesn't know I am. When she can't find me, she'll start checking out; then here I come with one little item to add to the basket.

Basically my rule about labels is that if the ingredients cover half a panel, there are too many. If the ingredients cover only two or three lines, I'll consider it. Five or six, you're pushing your luck. Two inches of fine type about all the ingredients in a package— I won't touch it. If it's a simple food and they have to have all that stuff in there to keep the package from falling in, I don't know if it's worth the trouble.

This ECKist approaches shopping the same way I do; he kind of gets lost in the aisles looking at all the food, doing useless things like reading labels. It's kind of fun, but if you've read one, you've read them all.

THE DENT MASTER

After the ECKist had finally finished his shopping, he ran outside, thinking, *I hope my car's OK.* Someone else was now parked on the left side of him. A car had gone, and this one had come. He checked both left doors carefully. They looked OK, so he got in the car and left. When he got home, he saw there was a big ding on the left side, not on the doors, but on the back quarter panel.

Gone were his big dreams of a car that wouldn't look a day older the day he finally sold it.

He knew he'd have to take his car to a body shop for repairs. They would fix the dent and repaint the whole back end. But he also realized it would be very expensive, so he decided just to drive the car for a while with the dent in it. From then on, the car didn't sing for him anymore. I guess the radio stations no longer had the magical music they did before. Or maybe he changed back to the old stations he used to listen to. I don't know. But the song was gone— just two months after he bought the new car.

The man told his friends, "It's foolish being so attached to a car. I'm going to get all the spiritual lessons out of this that I can." And so he let it go at that. But he was never quite happy again. He felt as if he'd let his car down: If he hadn't taken so long in the food store, his car would not have suffered the damage.

Two weeks after he found the ding in his car, the man took the car to the dealership for an oil change. As he was talking with the service manager, he mentioned the dent in the side.

"I just wondered," he said, "what's involved in getting this dent fixed?"

"It just so happens that there's this German fellow visiting," the service manager told him. "He fixes dings in cars all over the city; he goes from dealership to dealership. He has specially made steel tools, and he takes out the dents so you'd never know they were there."

This sounded really good to the ECKist. The service manager gave the ECKist the name of the German mechanic, and the ECKist sat down to wait for his oil change to be finished. But it seemed to be taking a very long time. The ECKist didn't want to be late getting back to work, and his lunch hour was nearly gone. He never cheated on his time; he always gave more than he took because he had an open heart.

People passed back and forth through the waiting room, including a man with windblown hair who

The man told his friends, "It's foolish being so attached to a car. I'm going to get all the spiritual lessons out of this that I can."

kept coming in to use the phone. Finally the service manager came in to tell the ECKist his car was ready. "By the way," he added, "there's the German fellow I was telling you about." And he pointed to the man with the windblown hair. "If you want, just go over there and ask him how much it would take to repair your car."

The man was working on a car, working with absolute concentration. He was taking a dent out of the side of the car, working very carefully with his special tools. He went in through the window on the inside with a long tool, and from the outside he'd occasionally tap the metal with a special hammer. Very gradually the dent disappeared. And even after it had disappeared, the mechanic worked on it for another twenty minutes.

The ECKist, who was watching, knew that the man was an artist, a master at what he did. He waited until the mechanic had finished, then he spoke.

"The service manager mentioned your name," he said. "I have a car out in the parking lot with a very sharp dent in it. I wonder if you'd have a look at it."

"I've already looked at it," the mechanic said. "I can fix it in a few minutes. It will cost you forty-five dollars." The ECKist was delighted, because that was far below what it would have cost had he taken the car to a body shop.

The two of them went outside to the car, and the mechanic started working. He made a very small hole in the wheel well, inserted his special tool, and began to hammer. After a while, the dent was no longer there. It had totally disappeared. In fact, it looked as if it had never been there. Yet for five minutes after the dent had disappeared, the master mechanic kept working. Then he closed the little hole he'd punched into the wheel well and touched it up with a little bit of paint.

"If you want it absolutely perfect," he said, "you'll have to take it to a body shop. They'll buff the area and reapply paint." But the dent didn't even show.

The ECKist asked the man where he had learned his art. "In a BMW factory in Germany," the man said.

The car owner realized that this man had taken what might appear to others to be a very low skill, and he had raised it to an art form. He was a master of the highest degree in fixing this sort of problem. And he was able to make a very good living from it.

He was a master of the highest degree in fixing this sort of problem.

GIVING UP AN ATTACHMENT

As we get older, we realize that our physical shape isn't what it used to be. We find we lose a step here and there; we just don't have the strength we once had. And we come to accept it.

The ECKist thought he had accepted this in himself, but when damage occurred to his car, it was almost as if he became depressed. Although he was detached about his body, he still had a very strong attachment to the condition of his car. When the damage occurred to it, he realized that he had a very limited ability to control conditions in his life.

But then he asked the Mahanta for help, and that's when the ECKist ran into the master mechanic.

The power of God is infinite.

He then realized that if you ask, and if it's part of your spiritual lesson—if something is there for you to learn—that nothing is outside of the power of God. The power of God is infinite. It reaches from one end of the universe to another, and it can certainly take care of something like a small dent in a car—in a way that is much more efficient than the way people usually fix such things.

The ECKist also had to give. But in his case, he had to give something up.

He had to give up his attachment to what he could do to make the world run his way. Because there are many times conditions are simply out of our hands. What do we do then?

If you have the gift of life, you have the greatest gift there is.

GIVING—THE SECRET TO GETTING

Most people pray to God.

But the ECKist didn't pray to God to fix things; he didn't ask the Mahanta to make things better. He realized that life itself is a gift. And if you have the gift of life, you have the greatest gift there is.

And so, as a spark of God, make the most of this gift. Do the best with what you have.

As I speak to you here, my function is merely to try to open your hearts to the real teachings which come later. I sit here and tell you about the principles of ECK. I tell you about giving, the secret to getting. You can also say, "Giving—the secret to receiving," but *getting* gets closer to it.

There's something I've seen again and again, which is a reflection of the spiritual darkness that is clouding the world today. People will lie, cheat, and steal to get something they haven't earned.

Victims, they call themselves. Victims. Because they do not appreciate the gift of life.

LEARNING CAUSE AND EFFECT

A businessman recently spoke about this subject. He said there are no victims. People complain to him that it's hard having a business. They never realized it was so difficult. He usually answers them, "Whoever said it was easy to make a living? And if you're going to make a better living, that's going to be even harder."

It's the Law of Cause and Effect. This is another name for karma.

Everyone thinks of karma as bad stuff that happens to you for the bad stuff you did. But karma is the good and the bad. In other words it's cause and effect, anything that occurs.

If you want something from life, you must first earn it. This is why I see a real problem, especially in the United States today, where political leaders are promising people something for nothing. The Law of Karma says if you are to receive something, you must pay for it in the true coin. Either people who make promises like this are lying, or they do not know the spiritual law. I think they do not know the spiritual law.

But in neither case should an initiate of ECK take something like this at face value. If someone tells you he's going to give you something free and easy, you'd better ask him, "What's it going to cost me?"

If he says it's not going to cost you much or anything at all, it's not true. Because the Law of Cause and Effect doesn't work that way. In the coming months and years, I'm going to have to get right back down to basics again and try to draw the relationship for you between cause and effect.

INHERITING HEAVEN

In the thirties during the depression people knew about this. There was even a saying: "There's no such thing as a free lunch."

But today many people feel they are entitled to other people's property simply because they ask for it. They believe that no effort needs to be made, that you can just have it for the asking. They think that all you have to do is get your leader in Congress or the Senate to put your pet project through. Then you'll live on easy street.

What kind of spiritual sickness are we talking about? This is the height of taking from life. People who do this will never have the love of God. Because they're not fit for it.

The meek shall inherit the earth, but the strong shall inherit heaven.

The meek shall inherit the earth, but the strong shall inherit heaven.

REALIZATION OF DIVINE LOVE

I leave this with you: The Law of Cause and Effect is, on one side, a training school, where we learn the lessons that life has to teach. If you want something of great value, you're going to have to work hard for it. There's no free lunch; there is no easy street.

When you learn the lessons, when you understand the Law of Cause and Effect, you graduate to the realization of divine love.

When you learn the lessons, when you understand the Law of Cause and Effect, you graduate to the realization of divine love. Your life becomes richer in the blink of an eye, because you have moved from the consciousness of the masses to the spiritual consciousness of God, of divine love.

You realize that you must pay your own way. And that anyone who tells you you're going to get a free ride is not being honest with you. Many people want to believe this sort of thing, and that's all right. But for those who are in ECK, in whatever way you can, realize that life itself is a gift. Do what you can.

I realize that many of you have worked years for your retirement benefits, and you deserve them. You need them because as you get older, you don't have the strength of youth. But you owe it to yourselves not to put your mind and your creativity on a shelf and just bungle along in life. Do what you can for yourself. Do what you can for others. In doing so, you are moving forward spiritually as a divine light of God.

I want to leave you with this: Move forward spiritually as a divine light of God. In the Light and Sound, may the blessings be.

ECK Worldwide Seminar, Los Angeles, California,
Friday, October 22, 1993

The great ECK Master Rebazar Tarzs told him that, in time, the God seeker finds within him this slow burning, long-lasting love for God.

2
THE SLOW BURNING LOVE OF GOD

*O*ften I tell stories, and I will again tonight. But I hope the stories never obscure from you the real reason for our being here: to open ourselves more to this burning love of God.

Sometimes the love of God burns so deeply and painfully that we feel life is too much to bear. We find ourselves in a paradoxical dilemma: having so much divine love that we don't know where to turn. People say they just want the love of God, but when it comes—when it truly comes—it burns deep, burns slow, and burns long.

THE SLOW BURNING LOVE OF GOD

Some people don't understand this. They feel the love of God is all sweetness and light—as indeed it is, at times.

But there are other times when this divine love has a nature that transforms anyone who is so fortunate as to have this blessing of God. Divine love will tear your insides out and replace them with something better.

Some may feel I'm overstating this. But anyone who has ever been touched by the burning love of God will realize that once this kiss of God has touched your heart you will never be the same. The effort then becomes to live in this world as a responsible human being. To go about your duties and to continue with your responsibilities while you are among people who have no idea at all about this deep love of God.

And you have to smile and laugh and cry with others. They never know or understand what they don't know and understand about divine love. You know and you understand, but you can't say. Because where are the ears to hear? Where is the heart to feel?

You find yourself in the worlds of God, surrounded by people, with the deepest sense of loneliness that you've ever felt. And you ask, "Is this the love of God?"

This is the paradox of God's love. It's at once the most wonderful fulfillment in your spiritual life and at the same time it leaves you apart from others, in a way, because few people have ever had this burning love of God.

Before you can receive you must give.

FEAR OF RECEIVING LOVE

Our theme this spiritual year is the Year of Giving. I would like to share some examples of the different ways of giving. Because before you can receive you must give.

We're always a little bit afraid to give of ourselves because someone may reject our gift. This, of course, hurts our feelings—especially if we have offered a gift that is very precious to us. To have someone refuse it hurts deeply. And so we are a little afraid to give.

Because of this fear, we find that we cannot receive. We wonder, *Where is the secret, and where is the key to receiving God's love?* Tonight I'll try to give you some indication of where to go and how to look for this love, this blessing of the Holy Spirit, so that it may enter your heart.

LEARNING TO LISTEN TO GOD

The Spiritual Exercises of ECK are simple contemplations; in a way they are the ECK equivalent to prayer.

Most people are used to prayers that ask something of God. They are used to telling God, "Do this for me. I want health. My finances aren't going very well; I need wealth."

Everybody's always telling God what to do. Then they wonder, *Does God get sick of listening? Why doesn't God ever do anything?*

In contemplation we shut our eyes, listen, and wait for God to speak to us. It's a whole different approach. Through the spiritual exercises and this contemplative effort we learn to listen to the Voice of God. The Voice of God is the Holy Spirit, which we call the ECK.

CHANGES FROM THE LIGHT AND SOUND

An ECK initiate was having a hard time with the Spiritual Exercises of ECK. She was not having the experiences she expected or was used to having. She wanted some meeting with the Light or Sound of God.

The Light of God may be yellow or blue or any of the other colors; It may look like a lamp, a spotlight, a flickering candle, or a lighthouse off in the distance. It may come as a soft glow, It may come as a piercing ray of light, or It may come as a bolt of lightning. It may come in any number of ways to your inner vision. But each time you see the Light of God, It will uplift you spiritually.

The Spiritual Exercises of ECK are simple contemplations; in a way they are the ECK equivalent to prayer.

It will make you in some way a different and better person than you were before.

The counterpart to the Light of God is the Sound of God. The sounds of nature mimic this Sound of God—birds or musical instruments; the sound of a train, a plane, rockets, or crickets; or some other sound like the high energy of a motor or an engine. Again, this is the action of the Voice of God working within you to leave you a little better, a little bit more purified spiritually than you were before the experience.

Each time you experience the Light and Sound of God, your point of view shifts a little bit.

GREATEST GIFT

Each time you experience the Light and Sound of God, your point of view shifts a little bit. Each time, it comes a little bit more in line with the spiritual, more in line with the Divine.

Your viewpoints will slowly change from those of people around you. In time you'll find it very difficult to understand why people even bother with prayers that constantly beg for something—as if life on earth entitles them to anything simply for the asking.

We have the greatest gift there is: the gift of life. And what we do from here on is up to us.

IMAGINATIVE TECHNIQUE

This initiate was trying to have more success with her spiritual exercises, and so she went into contemplation. She did an imaginative technique. In an imaginative technique, you shut your eyes and imagine something happening. You might imagine some scene where you're going to meet with the Inner Master, the Mahanta, the counterpart of myself in the dream or other inner worlds.

You try to make it an interesting experience of some kind. Something that is comfortable, peaceful, serene, if possible, because you want this exercise to work and you want to get rid of the problem of fear.

So she saw herself in a park, sitting on a bench, and a man came up to her. She couldn't see his face, but she knew it was the Master. She had picked some daffodils and handed them to the Mahanta. He in turn held open a little box and took a pendant from it.

The Key to Success

The pendant was shaped like a key, a large key that you might wear around your neck. At the base of the key was the ☾ symbol, and on the other end was the word *love.* The key meant: ECK opens the lock to love. After she had this experience, the woman said, "I've got to open my heart to love. Then I will have success with my spiritual exercises again."

Shortly after that experience, the woman had a dream. In the dream, she and several other ECK initiates went into a washroom to freshen up. A doctor came in behind them. He was very angry and very impatient. He went to a sink, turned the water on, but the tap was dry.

"You've broken the faucet," the doctor said to the women.

Then one of the ECKists went up to the faucet and turned it on. Water came flowing out. And someone said, "That is the way of ECK."

The lesson for the ECK initiate was that anger closes off the flow of God's love to you. But if you have love and trust in the Holy Spirit, the ECK, then the love of God will flow to you just the way water flows from a faucet.

Anger closes off the flow of God's love to you.

You've Got to Put Love into It

This dream was the second experience the woman had. The first was the imaginative technique which she mocked up. The third came through something we call the Golden-tongued Wisdom.

The Golden-tongued Wisdom is a blending of inner truths with an outer experience of some kind, some everyday activity that you're doing. This woman was knitting a sweater for an expected grandchild in the family. She had knitted this same sweater pattern for over forty years. She knew it by heart. She didn't really want to knit another sweater; she had made so many. Because her heart wasn't in it, as she knitted she would make mistakes, and she'd have to pull out the row of knitting and start over. This went on for a while. She'd knit some, make another mistake, and have to rip it out and knit the row all over again.

What's wrong here? she wondered. *Why can't I knit this pattern?* She was so familiar with it, she could practically do it in her sleep. And yet she was making mistake after mistake.

Finally she realized that she didn't really want to knit the sweater, and she wasn't putting her love into it.

If you want something to work—whether it's the spiritual exercises, a project at the office, a relationship, or anything else—you've got to put your love into it. Once the woman realized what was causing all these problems, she put her love and attention on knitting this sweater for the expected newborn. And from then on, the work went very quickly and easily.

If you want something to work, you've got to put your love into it.

IMPORTANCE OF HU

So often, we run into problems in our everyday life and things go wrong. And right away we think, *It's somebody else's fault.* If things go wrong, it's never us. If we would just take a moment to stand back and look things over, we would find that things are going wrong because of the way we are feeling that day.

We may be feeling angry, fearful, frenzied because of deadlines that we feel we can't meet, overworked, or anxious. The more anxious and upset we get, the worse our day goes. Suddenly other people are getting on our nerves and we're getting on other people's nerves. And at the end of the day, we go home exhausted. "I don't know how many more days like that I can stand," we say.

When your day is hard, remember to sing HU.

Very few people realize they caused this day themselves. Simply because they forgot to stop and chant HU.

HU, this name for God, can be very useful if you remember to sing it at a time like this. When your day is hard, remember to sing HU. It puts you back in line with the Holy Spirit.

ROCKETS

Another ECKist had a spiritual experience, but after the experience began, he then had to take it a step further. He had to give love to one of the ECK Masters, Rebazar Tarzs.

This initiate was doing the daily spiritual exercises, and suddenly he heard the sound of crickets. There weren't any crickets outside. So he just waited, staying with the experience. Suddenly it sounded as if a number of rockets were going off at the same time—a roaring, whooshing sound. It felt like he was in the center of a launching pad with rockets going off all around him.

The ECKist realized that this meant that he was moving into a higher state of consciousness.

This often happens. What you have to do then is stay calm. No harm will come to you, but you will have an experience that would be hard to explain to someone else who didn't know how the love of God works.

The teachings of ECK are to give you experience around the clock, twenty-four hours a day. While you are awake you get your experience in everyday life. And if you do your spiritual exercises, then when you go to sleep at night—maybe not every night but once every few weeks or months—you will have some inner travel that will expand your awareness. It will give you an entirely different view of life because of what you've seen and felt and known.

And in most cases you can't talk about it. Who are you going to tell?

LIKE-MINDED SOULS

So many of you—in one way or another, once or twice in your lifetime at least—have had some kind of experience that the average person hasn't had. These may be near-death experiences, out-of-the-body experiences, Soul Travel, astral projection, or seeing visions. In most cases, it's better that people don't have such experiences all the time. People who do are often not able to handle them. Generally, they are very much out of balance.

For most of you, these experiences come unannounced. Often they happen before you even hear about Eckankar. They make you wonder, *What happened to me? Am I going crazy?*

You ask people, "What happened?" You ask your

minister, but he doesn't know. You ask people you respect, people into philosophy or psychology or one of the medical arts. They don't know either. Maybe they've heard something about such things on television.

Then one day you're watching a television program, and you see that others have experienced this too. "All these experiences that these other people have been reporting are true," you say. And you wonder, *Where can I meet other people like this?* Often you can't. They're scattered all over the country, and the television program seldom gives out names and addresses.

But Eckankar is here again in the twentieth century. It's out in the open again. And one of the advantages of Eckankar and ECK seminars is that you can meet others who, in one way or another, have had experiences beyond what most people experience in life today.

One in every three Americans has had some kind of extraordinary spiritual experience—going out of the body or something of this nature. They may not have understood what it was, but they had the experience. We are here to help them. We're here to give them a frame of reference about what this experience means.

The Light and Sound are the Voice of God. They are to uplift you spiritually.

Eckankar is here again in the twentieth century. It's out in the open again.

The Light and Sound are the Voice of God. They are to uplift you spiritually.

GIVING LOVE TO THE ECK MASTERS

After this ECK initiate had the experience in his spiritual exercise where he heard crickets and the sound of rockets, he realized that he had to give more time to the Spiritual Exercises of ECK. He had to take them one step further.

When the experience began, he found himself out of the physical body and in the Soul consciousness. He was very aware; he knew that he could be anywhere in the universes just by wanting to be. You become the wish fulfilled. And the way you become the wish fulfilled is you think of something or someone that you very much want to see.

This ECKist wanted to see the ECK Master Rebazar Tarzs.

Rebazar Tarzs lives up in the Hindu Kush mountains, but most of his service is among people in the cities and in the crowds. He meets you where you need to meet him, when the time is right. And so this individual awoke on the other planes in full consciousness, in the Soul consciousness, out in the Soul body, and he found himself on the side of a steep mountain. First he saw the snow on distant mountaintops. And then he saw the nearby mountains.

He was standing on a ridge. He looked around, wondering, "Where is Rebazar?" And then he filled his heart with love, because he knew he had to give love if he wanted to take this experience a step further. So he just felt a strong, strong love for this ancient ECK Master.

There was the sound of footsteps off to the side, and coming along the ridge trail was Rebazar Tarzs.

THE FIRE OF GOD'S LOVE

"I'm happy to see you," Rebazar said. "Let's build a fire." It was cold. The ECKist looked around and found a few twigs from nearby bushes. He and Rebazar gathered a small pile alongside the ridge on this mountain. And Rebazar reached into his robe and pulled out a little bottle of paraffin. He poured this over the twigs and put a light to it. Immediately there was a bright flame.

If you ignite paraffin, it makes a brief, hot flame. But just as quickly as it starts, the fire dies out. After the flames died, only a few embers were left of the fire on the ridge trail.

As the ECK initiate watched, Rebazar Tarzs bent over this little fire and very carefully blew on the embers. Then he fed twigs into the fire, and very slowly they ignited. Soon there was a real fire going.

Rebazar Tarzs told him, "Often, when a person first comes into ECK, he has this strong hot flame of experiences. He will have many psychic experiences, and he will feel this is the real thing. But as they pass, as the mind forgets, the doubts return. And then the ECKist wonders, *Were those experiences real? Did these things really happen to me?*

"But the Master keeps blowing on these embers and uses the base of these experiences to build on. In time the ECKist, the God seeker, finds within him this slow burning, long-lasting love for God."

Often, when a person first comes into ECK, he has this strong hot flame of experiences.

FIRST EXPERIENCES

Some people don't understand the principle behind this story. They come into ECK, they have some fantastic experiences; and then if times change, if another Living ECK Master takes the leadership role, they say, "I used to have a lot more experiences with that other Master. This Master is false." But, you see, they don't have the knowledge or the wisdom to evaluate what their experience was in the beginning.

It was the hot, bright fire made with paraffin. When the flame burns out very quickly, these people become discouraged. Doubt sets in. If they get their history wrong and their chronology mixed up, they will attribute their experiences that they used to have to the wrong reason. And they'll feel they're right—no matter how much they are wrong.

This is why people who first come into ECK often have strong experiences, and then they seem to go into the background for a few years.

When they pick it up again, they are well balanced and stronger spiritually. You need to be spiritually strong to handle experiences with the Light and Sound of God. Too many too soon, and you become unbalanced—unfit to live in the world as a responsible human being.

You need to be spiritually strong to handle experiences with the Light and Sound of God.

YOU MUST GIVE LOVE TO GROW

If you look back, you become impatient. You say, "I'm not growing as fast as I used to. The teachings are not true anymore. The path has gone off in the wrong direction." You feel these are all the right reasons for your doubts. And I'm here to tell you that they're all the wrong ones.

You need to stay with the spiritual exercises. You need to give time to them. And when you give time to them, if it's right for you spiritually and a spiritual experience begins, then you must take it a step further. You must give love to someone or something. You must fill your heart with love.

I've said this as many different ways as I can. Because it's very important. Your ability to fill your heart with divine love depends on the strength of your desire for God.

Your ability to fill your heart with divine love depends on the strength of your desire for God.

Some people really do not want God. They want phenomenal experiences. They like to play with ghosts, with prophecy, and with the insubstantial things that belong to the shadow worlds.

They are not ready for truth. If truth came to them, they would not recognize it. And if you're not able to recognize truth, of course you can't accept it.

It's that old catch-22: You've got to unfold slowly into the consciousness of wisdom to accept wisdom.

A VISIT TO THE TEMPLE

At the ECK Summer Festival in Minneapolis, Minnesota, one of the ECK initiates from the East Coast was at the convention center downtown. But she felt a very strong need to go out to the Temple of ECK.

So she got on the shuttle bus, went out to the Temple, and visited the chapel. The chapel is small, maybe seventy or eighty seats; it's a place where you can contemplate. After she finished contemplating, the ECKist went outside and talked to some friends. She was watching the time because she had to catch a bus back to the convention center to be on the program later. But she heard a HU Song beginning in the sanctuary, so she went in there for a moment to sing HU with the other people.

And then she remembered her shuttle bus was leaving.

She ran outside, and the bus was disappearing down the driveway.

Oh, well, she thought, *I still have time to catch the next bus.* There was one more bus, but this one she couldn't afford to miss. She had a commitment to be on the program, and she wanted to be there.

"I'm going to be like one of these pillars," she joked with a friend, pointing to the pillars surrounding the Temple. "I'm not moving until the next bus comes." So she and her friend stood outside, waiting.

SUFI CABDRIVER

A cab was parked right out in front, and after a while the driver came up to them. It was summer, and it gets very hot in Minneapolis in summer. "I'm thirsty," the cabbie said. "Do you have some water I could get?" One of the initiates said, "If you go downstairs you can get some iced tea."

So the cabdriver went downstairs in the Temple where the refreshment center was set up, and he got himself something to drink. After a little while he came out and in his hand he had some ECK brochures. "HU is God?" he said. "HU is God for you too?" The man had a very thick accent, and the two women had a very hard time understanding him. But finally they said, "Yes. HU is a name for God for us too."

"Have you heard of Sufi?" he asked them.

"Yes, we've heard of Sufis," the women said.

And then he said, "Have you heard of Shamus?"

In ECK, we know of Shamus-i-Tabriz and his student Jalal ad-Din ar-Rumi. One of the ECKists said, "Oh, yes, and Jalal ad-Din ar-Rumi and his beautiful poetry."

The cabdriver said, "Not poetry, songs." Because to him these were love songs to God.

They talked a little while longer, and he said, "Do you know the summer dance?" By this time one of the two women had to go back to her duties inside the Temple and just this one ECKist was left. "What do you mean?" she said.

So he moved his hands, trying to express the whirling dervishes as they dance and go out of the body.

"Oh, you mean out of the body," she said. He said, "Yeah, out of the body. You know, HU, the summer

"HU is God?" he said. "HU is God for you too?"

dance, go out of the body."

And she said, "Yes, but we do it a different way. We sit in a chair and sing HU with our eyes shut."

They talked some more, and then his fare came. He helped the people into the cab, and before he left, he waved at her and he waved at the Temple. Then the Sufi cabdriver pointed at the Temple and said, "Sing HU."

There are other people in the world who have heard this name HU in different ways; sometimes they sing it. Singing HU is a way to lift yourself spiritually. A connection was made between the two women and the Sufi cabdriver, but first they had to offer him some refreshment, they had to give of themselves.

SUPPORT

Singing HU is a way to lift yourself spiritually.

An ECKist family went through some extreme difficulties in their community. They're very respected community leaders, working at high levels in the educational field in state government, but in their hometown the bias against the teachings of ECK was quite strong.

The wife works in a very responsible position as a school president. When she took the job, she expected people to be ethical. But there were jealousies. Some people were jealous that she, a woman from outside the state, had been named president. Other people who had been at the institution for years thought they had earned the right to have that position instead of her. And they used threats against her property and stuff of this nature to frighten her and her family, to try to break down her will.

But when she went to work each day and faced these people who were threatening her and lying to her, she kept trusting in the ECK, Divine Spirit, and she sang HU.

As the months passed, the community very slowly came forward to support her in her work. She was trying to make the educational institution as ethical and outstanding as it could be. A lot of decay and corruption within the organization came to the surface, just by her presence. But she's finally gaining support.

Before this seminar I was setting up appointments with different people, and I mentioned that I would like to meet with her and her husband. So we met last night. And early this morning she wrote me a five-page letter. She told a very interesting story.

THE WATCH STORY

Back in 1976, this woman attended the World Wide of ECK in Seattle, Washington. She was working as a seminar host, standing out in the lobby, when a bum came in off the street. He was a tall, swarthy person, and he just seemed to be there to make her day miserable.

She wanted to go into the main hall to listen to the talks. But the man wouldn't leave her alone.

At one point he even said, "Lend me some money so I can get some food."

The woman had a principle about not lending money to bums. She felt they would run off and buy alcohol or drugs with it, and she didn't like to contribute to that. But she decided to give this man something. She was getting her money out when the man suddenly reached into his own wallet, pulled out twenty dollars, and said, "I'll be right back. Got to get myself a hamburger."

Why'd he do that? the woman wondered, feeling really upset. She hoped the man was gone for good, but a few minutes later he came waltzing in the door, finishing up his hamburger. And he started playing games with her again.

Finally he sat down beside her and said, "That's a pretty watch. Give me your watch."

"What?" she said.

"Give me your watch," the man repeated.

The ECKist explained that her mother had given her the watch and she wasn't about to part with it. The man asked her a couple more times, and she refused.

"What's the matter, are you too attached to time?" the man asked her. And this of course bent her little mind into all kinds of little shapes. She didn't know what to say.

By this time, the woman had begun wondering, *Now is this an ECK Master or is this just a bum?*

Is This an ECK Master?

In the history of ECK, we have many cases of ECK Masters who appear in disguise to people to give them a blessing of God. But they will put the person to some kind of test. It's up to the person to either accept the love or reject it. Sometimes the test involves giving something small and receiving the love. In most cases, people usually reject the blessing of God that comes through one of these ECK Masters, because their disguises are very good.

When they leave, you're still not sure whether it was an ECK Master. A couple of weeks or months later, you may have an inner experience and see the Master in his full light. And he says, "I met you, and

In the history of ECK, we have many cases of ECK Masters who appear in disguise to people to give them a blessing of God.

I asked you for something. I asked you for a token, but you would not give it to me, when all I wanted to give you was the blessing of God."

The real learning then begins on the inner planes, because by the time the Master presents himself like this, the individual is just about ready to listen. The person has made one mistake, and he doesn't want to make another one in his dreams.

In ECK we get our experiences throughout the day, but they continue into our inner states at night through dreams or Soul Travel. In these inner experiences, someone comes to teach you about the wisdom of God and how you can make your life spiritually better in some way.

In ECK we get our experiences throughout the day, but they continue into our inner states at night through dreams or Soul Travel.

ONE MORE CHANCE TO GIVE

As the ECKist was wondering about this bum, a woman dressed in beautiful white clothes came over to them. She immediately went up to this bum and embraced him. *Why would anyone do that?* the ECKist wondered. And just then, an Indian family from England came up to the beggar, bowed down to him, and very reverently told this man their names.

What's going on here? Am I the only one missing something? the ECKist wondered.

The next thing she knew, the bum was halfway across the lobby. At the top of his voice, he shouted back at her, "Are you Jesus or Buddha? Who are you? Who are you truly, do you know? Or are you too attached to time?" And then he vanished.

Throughout the seminar, the woman looked for him everywhere, but she could not find this man. She was all torn up inside. It was as if her atoms had been completely taken out, replaced, and put back in a new way.

This happened back in 1976. Over the years she has told this story to her husband and children many times. At this seminar, the family was in a restaurant, eating, and in walked a bum, a very little guy. He walked around the room three or four times.

"I wish I had one more chance to give, because I missed the chance back in 1976," the mother said.

Her eleven-year-old daughter said, "What if he asks you for your watch, Mom?"

Mother said, "He wouldn't ask. It's not necessary now, because I'd give it to him."

The daughter said, "I'll take your watch." Kids, you know. And then she said, "Just kidding, Mom, just kidding."

The family got up, paid their bill, went out the door, and gathered themselves together to walk back to the hotel. As they were standing there, this little bum came out. He walked directly to the woman.

The man was trying to say something to her but it was as if he couldn't quite get the words out. "Uh, uh, I wonder if, uh, if I could ask, uh, you for a . . . ," he stammered. The woman felt all torn up inside again. *If he asks me for money, I know he's going to buy a bottle of booze or some drugs,* she thought. *I don't know if I can do it. No matter what I told my family.* She was really going through it. An unlit cigarette hung out of the bum's mouth, and he stood there as if he didn't know which way was up or down.

Finally he said to the woman, "I was wondering if you'd buy me a meal?"

This she could do, because she knew where the money was going. "Why, of course," she told him. So the husband reached into his pocket and gave her his wallet. She took the wallet and the bum into the restaurant, and she ordered this man a meal. "I want to pay for his meal," she told the cashier. "And let him have the change."

The man looked at her and said, "Well, thank you."

"I am very happy to do this for you," the woman said. And the little bum looked startled. "You are?" he said. She smiled. "Yes, I'm very happy that I could do this for you."

It took seventeen years for this whole experience to come full circle. It came about through many different ways and many different detours. And when the woman and her husband were called to come meet me last night, the whole story came out.

SPIRITUAL CONNECTION

There are people who met ECK Masters years before they came into Eckankar.

People feel that the ways of Divine Spirit are random, that there is no system or method to the ways of God, or that the path of ECK is not true. But there are people who met ECK Masters years before they came into Eckankar.

In some cases the individual doesn't know who these Masters are. But sometimes he or she does know these ECK Masters, even by name.

They are old friends lost over the years, people who used to teach truth and then disappeared while the individual went through his life experiences. And after the individual has gone through long trials and hardship, after life has softened him up to receive the pure teachings of Divine Spirit again, then he finds the teachings of ECK and the Mahanta, the Living ECK Master.

SHOW ME DIVINE LOVE

One day an initiate in Texas realized that he really didn't know much about divine love. So in his contemplation he asked the Mahanta, this inner side of myself, "Show me divine love."

Suddenly his dog walked up and licked him on the face.

It startled him. He was doing his spiritual exercises, and he had his eyes shut, trying to be very spiritual, asking a very important question, when his sweet dog walks up and washes his face. The dog had never done this before.

The man admits he's a very slow learner; he has a lot of doubts. For a while after this he wondered, *Was it a coincidence that the dog picked just this time to lick my face for the first time?* But it kept happening. In fact, his sweet dog friend walks up and washes his face for him every time he sits down to do his spiritual exercises.

This is how the Holy Spirit is bringing him the knowledge of what divine love is.

People feel it's OK for God to love them, and for them to love God. And if you have pets, you may know divine love is shared between you. But other people, who don't have pets and don't understand about divine love, might say, "Pets are pets. You like your pets, but you certainly would never call a person's love for a pet divine love. Are you kidding? Divine love for a dog, a cat, a bird?"

Divine love is something that is shared.

Divine love is something that is shared. In the same way it comes from God to people, it is shared from people to people, from people to pets, and from pets to people. It works very simply. Divine love doesn't have the barriers that the human mind makes.

God's love doesn't make divisions or separations like this, but the human mind does.

HEART OVER MIND

We are so proud of this vaunted human mind. We're proud of this thing that is filled with biases, doubts, confusion, fear, anger, guilt, and greed. We are very proud of this instrument of ours, encased in this little shell and covered with fuzzy stuff. We're very, very proud of our minds.

But so often it's our mind itself that is the block that keeps us from God and God's love. The people who are very intellectual have the hardest time in finding God.

From what I've seen, people who don't have great intellectual capacity find it very easy to love God, their fellow beings, and their pets. It's very easy for them. Why? They're not encumbered by this great piece of machinery up in the attic.

You have to be the master of your mind. And what part of you is the master of the mind? It has to be the heart.

You have to be the master of your mind. And what part of you is the master of the mind? It has to be the heart.

FINDING THE MEANING OF LOVE

This initiate who got licked on the face by his dog wasn't convinced yet, being a slow learner and all. So one day he was helping some friends clean up his yard. There were some empty soda cans behind the house, and a woman was collecting them. To the man, she looked maybe one cut above a bag lady, the female equivalent of a hobo. There's a difference between bums and hobos. Hobos will work for their food, bums just want the food for free. This bag lady was willing to work, so she was collecting cans, and she had a little dog with her.

The ECKist was in the backyard doing some other things, and he saw the little dog and talked kindly to it. He called it over, and the dog came very carefully. It sniffed at his hand and stood to get petted. And then the woman came over, and they talked a little bit about one thing or another.

As he was about to leave, the ECKist looked into the woman's eyes. They were so clear and sincere. As a matter of fact, so were the dog's eyes.

He realized that this woman had a special love for her dog, and the dog had a special love for her.

"Thank you for being so kind to my dog," the woman said. The woman loved the dog, and probably no one in society loved her except the dog.

Here comes this ECKist, who is trying to find the meaning of love. He finds it in himself to approach the woman through her dog, and he was kind to the dog. This in turn allowed him to give and receive love from this old bag lady.

During the next few days when the ECKist did his spiritual exercises, he tried to focus his attention on different things, but the face of this woman and her little dog always came back to him. This woman's face was always on his inner vision. And after a few days, he realized that this was divine love, this was the love that God was showing him.

It's a very humble love; the love of God is often very low where no one will look for it. And this is why so few people find it.

It's a very humble love; it's a true love. Don't look too high, because you won't find it. The love of God is often very low where no one will look for it. And this is why so few people find it.

I would like to remind you that if times are hard for you during the day, try to spiritualize yourself by singing HU. But sing it with love for God. This will lift you and help you through. It will make you a better person, in all ways and in all places, for all beings.

ECK Worldwide Seminar, Los Angeles, California, Saturday, October 23, 1993

One woman said, "The second time you chanted HU, I heard and saw a freight train right here in this room."

3

LOVE
DRIVES SOUL ON

*A*s I prepare my talk, I try to see what you will need most spiritually. I'll put certain material together, and when the talk begins I have a vague idea of what is going to happen.

Then sometimes, the ECK changes things. It wants the same material given out but in a very different tone. I thought last night's talk would be a very light one. It turned out to be entirely different. This is always quite a surprise to me too.

I prepare the material, realizing it has to fit into so much time, but other things get added. We go on for a while, and I happen to look at my watch. *It's about time to do onstage edits here and see what we can cut out,* I think. So then I have to go through my notes, quickly edit in my head, and try to make up the time difference.

It gets very interesting as I scramble about, trying to give you whatever you need most spiritually— and many other things get added in. I don't have a lot of say in how it goes, frankly.

LOVE DRIVES SOUL ON

On Sunday morning at a seminar, I usually like to focus on a topic that has to do with the membership of ECK—those of you who care about the ECK missionary work—or knowing how to get along better with your family and friends. Like many of you, I came from a Christian background. Sometimes our family and friends do not understand this love that comes to us not of our conscious asking.

At some point in our spiritual journey, we find the teachings of ECK. In my case, I did not want to disrupt anything at home. If I had had a choice I would've remained in the church that I grew up in.

I would've just stayed there because it was comfortable. I had the friendship and good opinions of all the people I had known since youth.

But divine love drives us on.

YOUR OWN EXPERIENCE OF DIVINE LOVE

You come into ECK with a new understanding, one that came out of the blue, so to speak. And it won't let you rest. An inner experience—or two or three or four—has come along and given you a different viewpoint about God.

And it's yours. Nobody has told you about it, nobody has impressed it upon you. It's your own.

An experience with the Light and Sound of God will change you. Divine love will compel you to make changes in your life. Otherwise you cannot live in peace.

Divine love will compel you to make changes in your life. Otherwise you cannot live in peace.

The trick is to live your beliefs while allowing others to continue with theirs. What's even harder is trying to live your beliefs when your family and friends don't want you to have your beliefs. That can be very, very difficult.

WHEN SOMEONE MOVES ON

Some of the people I've known in ECK have gone back to their original religion or to another religion. They got as much as they wanted from the ECK teachings in a year or a month or however long they were with Eckankar. They wanted to go somewhere else where they felt more comfortable.

Our teachings are built on spiritual freedom. If someone wants to leave, I let them leave. I don't say a word.

It's similar to something I learned in the work world. Let's say people work for a company and they want to leave. I found it's best to ask them why, to find out the reason. There may be something a manager can do to overcome some small problem. But if they want to leave, it's best to let them leave. Don't talk them out of it. Sooner or later they're going to leave anyway.

Managers like to keep their good employees; they do not like good workers to go. But if this inner urge comes to a person, if he says, "I have to be moving on," and he feels strongly about it, just let him go. These people are answering their inner voice. However it comes—by intuition or feeling or whatever—they feel they need to be somewhere else, and so they must go.

Our teachings are built on spiritual freedom.

YOUR FREEDOM AND OTHERS' FREEDOM

These are the worlds of ECK, or Holy Spirit. If I want to go somewhere, I would like to have the freedom to go there. And if I want this freedom for myself, I must be willing to allow it for other people. They must have the same freedom. According to the Law of Karma, if I'm not willing to allow another the freedom to come and go, then I lose my freedom to come and go.

This is why the spiritual path is a very exacting path. It truly means you must do unto others as you would have them do unto you. It really means that.

When a prized employee says he's leaving, right away the employer thinks of his own inconvenience. This is human nature. He remembers all the time it's taken to train this person and how good a worker he is. But if the inner call of that person says it's time to move on, that person's going to move on.

He may stay two or three months longer, but that inner call is going to come again. And eventually the employer is going to have to meet the inconvenience.

So it's best to just ask for a reasonable time to make the transition, enough time to find someone to replace the employee. It's best to say, "I respect your wishes. How much time can we have? How long will you stay to train the new employee?" This is reasonable, because this is also a part of the spiritual life. It's a matter of responsibility to make sure that we don't create vacuums when we leave.

There is such a thing as self-responsibility. But no one person can draw that line of self-responsibility for another.

BLOWING WITH THE WIND

Some people think freedom means just blowing with the wind. If the wind comes from the west, you go east; if it comes from the south, you go north. No. There is such a thing as self-responsibility. But no one person can draw that line of self-responsibility for another.

No one person can say, "This is how you must be responsible." It doesn't work that way.

If the person leaves without notice, the employer may never hire a person like that again. And the person may find out that whatever he thought was so great out on the other side of the fence, where the grass was supposedly greener, wasn't. Then he comes to get his job back. The employer may say, "I may not want to hire someone who's always flitting around."

Some people look like adults, dress like adults, and talk like adults, but they are emotional and spiritual children. And who can afford to hire a child?

Such people don't understand that you've got to make commitments, and if you make a commitment, you keep it. You may change your mind, but you always give proper notice. And if you've given proper notice, and you've done everything that you have agreed to do, then go. Go in freedom.

You're not burning your bridges behind you. If you ever want to come back, the employer will be very happy to have you back, because you did things in a responsible way.

Love drives Soul on. So, you see, there's more to freedom than simply reacting to whims.

LISTEN TO YOUR INNER VOICE

Not everything in life allows you to make very careful, drawn-out plans, though. Things can change suddenly, and you have to change with them. But when you have a chance to plan, then you plan.

Again, there is no line in the sand that anyone can draw. There is no line that says, "This is where responsibility ends and freedom begins." There is no such line; you have to decide that for yourself. And according to the Law of Cause and Effect, experience will teach you if your decision was good or not.

Your own experience will say, "You made a good decision" or "You made a bad decision." That's what life is about. It's all about decisions of right and wrong. *Shall I do this, shall I do that?* you wonder. And if

*Always listen
to your
inner voice.*

you do this, the fears come: *What's going to happen?*

But if you say, "I cannot stay any longer," whether it's as an employee, as a member of a religion, or even as a chela of Eckankar, listen to your inner voice.

Always listen to your inner voice.

A NEW KIND OF ECK MISSIONARY

Back in the 1970s an ECKist in Minnesota named Jim had been full of missionary zeal. It was the kind of zeal that is very easy to criticize in other groups.

For example, we criticize Christian missionaries who went into South and Central America and destroyed the native culture shortly after the time of Columbus. We look back and say, "Those missionaries did a lot of damage." Every religion has its dark side. Every religion also has its bright side where it has uplifted the people it came to serve.

*Every religion
has its bright
side where it
has uplifted the
people it came
to serve.*

In the 1970s, Jim and some friends went to a small town in a neighboring state where he had grown up. They put on talks about ECK, they had meetings in parks. It was a conservative town, but when it came to religious matters, people there seemed to be open to new ideas.

To Jim and his friends, it seemed to be a very natural place for people to learn about Eckankar. But they used all the wrong methods. They were pushy, they didn't have any grace back then. It's part of learning.

BECOMING RESPONSIBLE

Eventually, Jim and most of the others moved away. And life went on. Jim got married, he had a family, and his life changed.

If you aren't responsible before you have kids, you

become responsible. You've got to find a school for them, you've got to get a job to keep them clothed. They're always wanting baseball gloves and uniforms for Little League, so you've got to take care of all that. Pretty soon fifteen or eighteen years have passed, and you realize you've become an entirely different person.

You've become a responsible member of society while you were busy taking care of the needs of your family, trying to make the paycheck stretch far enough to cover the food, the clothes, and the home.

SIMPLE HELP

Jim recently spent some time in his childhood town again. As a casual thing he thought he would like to tell people about Eckankar.

So he put a little ad in the paper: "Dreams, Soul Travel, and ECKANKAR," inviting people to a public meeting on a certain date, at a certain time. He didn't think twice about it.

A young reporter from the local paper happened to see the ad for the ECK talk, and on the day of the talk the reporter called Jim. He seemed very interested in Eckankar after reading the ad. So he interviewed Jim, Jim's wife, and another ECKist. The interviews appeared in a very good article on Eckankar.

Everybody in town saw this article, except Jim and his family. For some reason, they were busy working, and they never got to see the article before a family get-together that was planned for the next weekend. At the family outing, not one of the relatives said one word about the article. Everyone was very, very quiet about it.

The article appeared the same night as the talk

on Eckankar, and four people came: a Native American woman with her two children, and the reporter. Jim began talking about dreams, Soul Travel, and Eckankar. As he gave his introductory talk, the woman sat there very quietly and patiently and listened.

When the talk was over, the reporter, curious, asked the woman, "Why did you come?" And the ECK initiate was curious too. Was it because of dreams?

No, the woman said, it wasn't because of dreams. It was because her life was so hard. She had heard about HU, this ancient name for God, and she hoped it was something to help her in her very hard life.

Jim said, "I think I missed something in my talk."

He had talked about dreams and Soul Travel, but he didn't realize that this woman had come to fill a great spiritual need. Her outer life was so hard that she was at her wit's end. She didn't know what else to do. So Jim told her about HU, something to try for help in her daily life. She could sing this love song to God.

Afterward, Jim got to thinking, and he realized he had learned a valuable lesson.

TEACHING OTHERS HU

In Eckankar, it doesn't matter if you make a mistake. You just have to accept responsibility for it. Actually, you have to do more than accept responsibility for it. When you accept responsibility for something, it means that you're going to learn from your mistake and next time try to do better.

The next time Jim gave an ECK talk, ten women came from the Christian community plus one ECKist friend of his. The women were very quiet; they mostly listened.

At one point, Jim said to his ECKist friend, "We

could demonstrate the HU." The women had nothing against that, so they all sang HU.

When they finished, one of the women said, "What did you expect when you sang HU?"

Jim said, "I always listen for the Sound of God."

The Sound of God is reflected, or echoed, in the sounds of nature. It can be anything: the sound of buzzing bees, the sound of birds. These sounds of nature are a reflection of the many different Sounds of God that exist in the natural order.

The Sound of God is reflected, or echoed, in the sounds of nature.

Another of the women said, "It's very funny, but the first time you chanted HU, nothing happened. The second time you chanted HU, I heard and saw a freight train right here in this room."

People think that the Holy Spirit speaks to us in the human voice. This can occur, but it usually happens when a messenger of God—an angel, for example—is sent to a human being. Then people hear a voice. But the pure Voice of God is music, the Audible Sound Current, the Holy Spirit.

The pure Voice of God is music, the Audible Sound Current, the Holy Spirit.

It is the sound of HU, because all sounds in nature are incorporated into this sound HU. All the sounds in this room. For instance, as we sit here there's the sound of the air conditioner and the hum of the speakers. Back home, sometimes if you're by yourself chanting HU, and the air conditioner's running or the refrigerator's running, you'll find it very interesting: the sound of the air conditioner or the refrigerator seems to be in harmony. As you sing the song of HU, it just seems to fit all the sounds around.

Jim wanted to tell this woman so many things—about how this Sound of God was uplifting her spiritually, how it was opening her ears to hear and her eyes to see. But he didn't. He had learned a lot since he was the rash young man back in the midseventies in his hometown. He realized the woman had to have the interest to take the next step herself.

If she really cared about truth and the wisdom of God, she would look further into the teachings of ECK. Then God would give her the wisdom she was prepared to receive. Jim's function was simply to be there, to provide the opportunity as he had at the talk. And these women had taken the first step—by coming.

TAKING THE STEPS YOURSELF

So often we think God's gifts come simply because we ask. For instance, we're in the privacy of our home, and we pray, "God, give me wisdom."

But sometimes God requires that you go out into the world. In other words, you have to stand up, put one foot in front of the other, and go look for wisdom, divine love, understanding, or whatever you're seeking. You have to be willing to go outside of yourself.

You have to give up some of your preconceived ideas about what God is, what divine love is. It means having the attitude of a child.

TEACH ME THY WAYS

Children have so little experience in this world. They pretty much accept things at face value.

This can be a danger and a risk because they don't know there is danger on the street. So their parents have to teach them and show them.

But as a mature spiritual being in a path, church, or religion, maybe you feel that there is something more. In looking for this, you're going to have to use all the experience that you have gained as an adult— about how to be careful, about not getting cheated and misled—and at the same time, you're going to have to be able to open your heart like a child. You're going to have to say, "Teach me. Teach me thy ways."

Divine truth is not apparent. It is not obvious. It's like pearls before the swine. The pearls are there, but people cannot see them unless in their hearts and minds they are ready to receive the gifts of God.

Divine truth is not apparent. It is not obvious.

ACCEPTING GOD'S LOVE

What prepares you for the true path of God? The experiences of life.

You might think it's a holy book, like the Bible or *The Shariyat-Ki-Sugmad.* But what really prepares you for the true path of God is the experiences you have. This is what determines your capacity to accept the love and wisdom of God.

What prepares you for the true path of God? The experiences of life.

When times are hard, some people complain. And as they complain about the hard times, they shut themselves off from the opportunities that lie within their troubles.

Other people have learned to be patient. They look for the lessons within their hardships or troubles.

This is what I'm trying to show you as members of Eckankar: Whenever troubles come up, don't say, "Why me?" as if you're the only one who's ever had troubles! Everyone has troubles. If you are on earth, you have troubles. This very small attitude—that you have the worst troubles—means that you're just kidding yourself. But even worse, it means you're shutting yourself off from the Voice of God.

WHY IS EXPERIENCE IMPORTANT?

When trouble comes, realize that you ultimately have created that problem for yourself, according to the Law of Karma, the Law of Cause and Effect. You created this problem for yourself because of a lack of knowledge of the ways of divine law.

The way to get this knowledge is not through a holy book or scripture. Scriptures can be guidelines. They can give you a clue of what life is all about, what the spiritual laws are. But ultimately it gets down to testing these laws in your daily life.

In other words, you have to experience life in order to grow spiritually. There is no other way.

Once you realize this, you won't be so quick to point your finger at someone else who seems to have no order or control in his life. You won't be so quick to say, "That person's made such a mess of his life. What a sorry human being. God's love must really be great to even let that person be on earth." That sort of attitude is the height of arrogance. And such an attitude may not be right on the surface. We're too cordial and civil for that. But the attitude is still parked way down there in the left pocket somewhere, where we think, *Boy, those people sure don't know how to run their lives. There but for the grace of God go I.*

We have our complaints and our problems and troubles, and it never occurs to us that our troubles are just as easy for other people to solve as their troubles are for us to solve.

You begin by chanting HU. You begin by singing this love song to God.

We're very wise about other people and often very foolish and ignorant about how to make our own lives better.

HOW TO BEGIN

How do you begin? I try to make this as easy as possible. You begin by chanting HU. You begin by singing this love song to God. Why? Because it opens your heart. It opens your heart to the Light and Sound of God.

When I say that the way to divine wisdom and understanding comes through experience, I'm talking about more than just outside experience, such as you might get at work, at home, or in the family. I'm speaking about the spiritual experiences you get during the Spiritual Exercises of ECK.

THE TAROT-CARD READER

One of the new members of ECK in Australia used to be with the Rosicrucians. The Rosicrucians are a fine group; they try to teach people self-responsibility. In the days before she came to ECK, this woman was a tarot-card reader. She was always very careful to talk to her clients about cosmic law as she understood it from the Rosicrucians.

As she read their cards, she would say, "I'm just giving you possibilities. It's up to you to choose from among these possibilities and take responsibility for the ones you choose in order to try to improve your life."

This was in 1989, as she was just about ready to find out about the teachings of ECK. She was already learning that some of her clients chose very selectively from her readings and kept the very worst as guidelines and goals. By visualization on their part, they actually created a very bad future for themselves. Afterward, they always came complaining to her.

We don't get into tarot-card readings in Eckankar; they are part of the psychic arts. It's OK before you get to Eckankar, but by the time you come here there are higher ways to look for wisdom and ways of guiding your own life.

The woman realized that something was wrong. She was giving people a fair reading. But as she tried to give these people guidance to make their own lives better for themselves, those who were down on life picked the things out of her readings that would hurt them. And they did it with uncanny accuracy.

They would always call her back and let her know how their life had gone so wrong since they had listened to her.

Eventually the woman got tired of this. When you're getting enough experience of a certain kind, you begin to see the same pattern evolving. She saw these people were making her responsible for their own decisions.

Finally, she wanted no part of it. Then she came into Eckankar.

SERVING LIGHT AND SOUND

Not long after, one of her former clients called her. She wanted another tarot-card reading. The ECKist explained she was no longer doing that. She said she was now in Eckankar and that every Thursday she volunteered at the ECK center. It was her day to keep the center open for visitors.

"Wonderful," the client said. "Thursday is my day off."

So now the two women meet on Thursdays. The ECKist was happy to be able to tell someone else about the teachings of ECK, and the ECK had something for her former client to learn about the Light and Sound of God. The ECKist feels happy just to be able to serve in this way.

WE LOVE GOD TOO

Our neighbors and relatives are good people. But if there is something they do not understand, they often become the way most people get when there is something unknown in their lives. They become fearful. And they strike out in anger and do all kinds of foolish things which are less than spiritually responsible.

In ECK, we learn about the sensitivities of other people, that they're only human too. They may not take the time to learn what the teachings of ECK are about. They may not know that we love God too.

In Eckankar, we try to carry it to the next level. We try to let other people love God too.

This is the next step, a better form of religion. It is letting other people love God in their own way. Sometimes this is the hardest lesson to learn.

In Eckankar, we try to let other people love God too.

A better form of religion is letting other people love God in their own way.

FEAR OF SHARING ECK

A woman named Mary had had a hard time telling other people about the teachings of ECK. She was with a group of women who helped each other through their times of trouble. And they had met for three years on Saturday morning.

The eight women had become very close friends. But Mary was hesitant about telling them about the teachings of ECK.

The women knew most everything about each other in every other way. But Mary never talked too much about Eckankar. In fact she didn't talk about it at all to them. And if neighbors asked what religion she belonged to, she found a way not to talk about it. Because of this fear: What would people do? How would they treat her once they found out she didn't belong to a mainstream religion?

I never would have ever believed that there was this kind of bias against religions in America when I was still a Christian. I would never have believed it. But many of you who have come from different religions and philosophical groups in America and around the world find that people are people and they have their dark little fears. And it doesn't make any difference what religion you're from. You can expect this if you are a member of a minority group. And if you're a member of a minority group such as Eckankar, you had better learn to be sensitive toward other people, until they learn how to let others love God too.

Mary was just about ready to leave this group, so in the second-to-last meeting she brought some ECK brochures to share.

She had decided to share the teachings of ECK with them, because these teachings were the most important thing in her life.

They asked her, "What has the ECK done in your personal life?"

As she was telling them about Eckankar and all the different things connected with it, she was very surprised at how they were pulling the information from her. She didn't have to push it at them; they wanted to know. They asked her, "What has the ECK done in your personal life?" So she began to speak about dreams, past lives, and other things; how the teachings of ECK had changed her; and how ECK had given her a greater insight into who she had been and who she is today.

OPEN HOUSE

Mary hadn't ever mentioned anything about the teachings of ECK to her group because three of the eight women were very devout Christians. She did not want to offend them or cause anything to get in the way of their friendship.

But at this meeting, Mary told the women that there was an open house at the Temple of ECK, and she had brought invitations.

One of the Christian women came to the Temple of ECK open house, which surprised Mary a lot. Another of the Christian women had joined a group that was practicing kundalini yoga. She had gotten in a little bit over her head and didn't realize what she was dealing with. This woman called Mary one night and said she was going out of balance and she didn't know how to get herself back to earth. She was losing it, and she was scared. So Mary told her about HU and how to sing this name for God.

HU would help, but in a case like this I might have also suggested, "Don't do the kundalini yoga anymore. Because you have to build up to that sort of thing. You have to come from a culture where this is as much a part of the culture as prayer is part of the Christian culture. You have to grow up in it. Otherwise you could be in for some trouble."

The third of the strong Christian women was very interested in past lives. Can you believe it? So Mary learned something here. She realized that she didn't have to be afraid.

She could just let other people know she was in Eckankar, and they would ask her about it.

COOKING CLASS

Mary is also a gourmet cook, and she teaches cooking classes. She had an assistant who was helping at this cooking class about a year ago, a young woman whose name was Rebecca. She was a very fine person. Mary and Rebecca got along very well.

One evening after they had finished a class, Rebecca happened to ask Mary, "Where are you coming from? Why are you the way you are?"

So Mary took a chance and said, "I'm a member of Eckankar."

Rebecca wanted to know all about it, and Mary said, "I'll send you an *ECKANKAR Journal*." So Mary did. And then she didn't see Rebecca for many months. Mary wondered, *Have I in some way pushed the teachings of ECK upon my cooking assistant?* Had she done this unwittingly? Because Mary certainly had no intention of doing it. She didn't even want to talk much about ECK.

About a year later, Rebecca again volunteered to be her assistant in a cooking class. During the class, Mary noticed that her friend was a little bit more upset than usual, less fun-loving and laid-back. She even got irritated at some of the people who had come to the class and were trying to learn how to cook. Rebecca seemed to be on edge about everything. So when the class was over and Mary and Rebecca were cleaning up, Rebecca began to talk about her life. She'd been going through a rough time.

Rebecca had lost her job and was having a hard time financially, but she kept asking about ECK. Friday nights, she had been watching videos on Eckankar on the local cable station. And she had found them very interesting. She'd enjoyed the talks about ECK.

Mary suddenly realized that Rebecca's troubles had begun when Mary had sent her the *ECKANKAR Journal* a year earlier.

A PILE OF KARMA

What was happening? Rebecca's karma, this little pile of karma that's always just lying around underfoot, needed to be walked through. Rebecca had tripped over her own karma for a little while.

When you begin with the teachings of ECK, this purifying Light and Sound of God begins to flow into your heart. If you have this little pile of karma that's just been lying around, you probably have to work through it. And you find things a little rough for a little while.

I have to be honest with you. This is part of the reality of the spiritual path. You're going to meet yourself.

These are not troubles that are caused by somebody else or ones that have just hit you for no known reason. There is a known reason, and it is your own lack of knowledge about the laws of God, the laws of life. When you don't know the laws of life you break them. And as you break these laws, the Law of Cause and Effect says, "You must pay for them."

This is why the teachings of ECK are extremely honest. Nobody else tells you if you are living up to a certain spiritual standard or not. Your behavior tells everybody where you are spiritually.

This is part of the reality of the spiritual path. You're going to meet yourself.

Your behavior tells everybody where you are spiritually.

EAGLES IN ECK

Some people who have high initiations are betraying themselves because they do not have the moral and ethical character to live up to those initiations. I don't like to say this, but it's true. Other people who are not members of ECK are five or ten years ahead of some Second Initiates in ECK. They have come into this lifetime much further along on the path to God.

I like to look at people as people. Whether or not you are a member of ECK or another church or religion doesn't make any difference. If you're a good person in Eckankar, you would be a good person in Christianity, and vice versa.

I like to be around good people. I do not like to be around people who try to cheat me, steal from me, or lie to me. I'm very much the way you are in this.

We like to have people around us who bring out the best in us. Especially if we are looking for the highest in life, especially if we are looking for the love and the truth of God. It's the old thing of birds of a feather flocking together. If you're an eagle, you want to be around eagles.

Love God, and let others love God in their own way too.

HOME IN THE HEART OF GOD

I would like to thank you for having seen the richness and the potential of coming to the seminar. As you go back out into life, remember to keep in balance. That means doing your duty to your loved ones, getting along with those who do not share your beliefs in ECK.

Love God, and let others love God in their own way too. Set the example of what it means to be a lover of God.

I leave you with this thought: If you would have love, you must first give love. And if you give divine love to others, you shall have divine love for yourself.

So as you make your way home, back to your homes here and back to your home in the heart of God, I am always with you.

ECK Worldwide Seminar, Los Angeles, California,
Sunday, October 24, 1993

HU is ancient. When they come back to ECK, it's the name people recognize from other lifetimes.

4

THE PATH TO GOD

*E*ckankar is the Religion of the Light and
Sound of God.

The Light and Sound are the two aspects
of God that speak to the human race, that
speak to each Soul. The Light and Sound together
are the Voice of God, what the Old and New Testaments call the Holy Spirit or Logos. Together, they
are simply divine love.

ROLES OF THE MASTER

*You are the present Living ECK Master of
Eckankar, and you also embody the Mahanta Consciousness. Could you explain these two roles?*

People talk about the Mahanta Consciousness as
being something that you slip off and on like a shirt.
But, in fact, the person who takes on the role of
spiritual leader and has a certain level of spiritual
growth then becomes both the Mahanta and the
Living ECK Master; which means the Mahanta is
the inner side of the teacher and the Living ECK
Master is the outer side of the teacher.

This gives a balance of both the inner and outer
teachings so that the individual can have a clear,
unobstructed path back home to God.

*The Light and
Sound are the
two aspects of
God that speak
to the human
race, that speak
to each Soul.*

HOW IS THE NEXT MASTER CHOSEN?

How is the Living ECK Master chosen, and has the next one been chosen yet?

The Living ECK Master is always chosen by God. (In ECK we call God *Sugmad.*) And there is a circle of candidates who are in training for the position of spiritual mastership.

Sometimes they move forward spiritually, then they move backward, then they move forward again. This process can go on for years until the final moment when the successor to me is chosen, and at that point, God chooses the person and I will tell others who this person is. I will tell them in one way or another, either personally or by written record.

The Living ECK Master is always chosen by God.

BLENDING OF INNER AND OUTER

Is the Mahanta Consciousness always with you?

It's like this: I am the Mahanta. That means I am the Inner Master and I am the Outer Master. Let's state this question another way: to say, Is the Mahanta Consciousness always with me? is like saying Is the outer consciousness always with me? Yes, it becomes a part of you, that you are not just the Mahanta Consciousness.

In this case, I'm saying about myself, "I'm not just the consciousness" as if it's something apart from me. I am the Mahanta because this is the blending of the inner and the outer worlds in physical form.

WHAT MAKES ECKANKAR UNIQUE?

There are so many choices available to the seeker of truth today, including various teachings of the Light and Sound. What makes Eckankar different?

There aren't that many teachings about the Light and Sound. There are a lot of teachings that know nothing about either the Light or the Sound as an important part of the spiritual path.

Christianity speaks about the Light in a number of places in the scriptures. For instance, Saul on the road to Damascus—that was the Light of God. But I don't think Christianity understands the full importance of the Light of God. And even those few religions that do have both the Light and Sound of God may not fully understand the importance of having both of them as a part of a viable spiritual path.

So, in ECK we teach that there is this balance of the two aspects so that people can have the straightest, most direct, and most spiritually beneficial path to God.

VALUE OF HU

HU is the main mantra used in Eckankar. It has also been used in other spiritual traditions in the past. What makes this one-syllable word so powerful?

It's powerful because it's the ancient name for God. It's a name that some of the Eastern religions are aware of, but in the West it's pretty much an unknown name. And it is much more effective as a love song to God than just the simple Anglo-Saxon word *God*.

HU is ancient. When they come back to ECK, it's the name people recognize from other lifetimes. When they come back to ECK, they're going to remember. They're going to find help in their lives when using it, when singing it, because it makes a connection all the way back through the earliest times when people came to this planet. People who reincarnated a long

HU is ancient. When they come back to ECK, it's the name people recognize from other lifetimes.

time ago have this unconscious knowledge of it. And the ones who have been here before many times love the sound.

SPIRITUAL TRAINING

Where and how does the student of ECK receive his or her spiritual training?

The spiritual training for the ECK initiate begins before the person even becomes a member of Eckankar.

For instance, some people grow up as a member of a Christian group, like the Episcopal Church. Then a few years later they may become Lutherans, perhaps. Then they'll go along a little farther and find themselves members of the Unity Church. And then as they progress in this life, after many hardships and experiences, they finally realize that they are looking for something else.

The religions of the past have not helped them fulfill the yearning for love, divine love, that's in their heart. And they come into ECK. They have then taken the first big step in their journey back home to God.

The journey home to God is what life is about. In a sense it's not even a journey, it's an ongoing experience. But it does have to do with direction, because until a person finds the teachings of ECK, he is carried on a great wave from God that goes all the way out into the universes.

As soon as you hear about ECK and accept its principles and teachings of divine love, you catch the return wave home. This is why it's such an important teaching for people who may come to the critical juncture in their life where they are serious about

The journey home to God is what life is about.

doing something more with their own life than they have been able to do so far through other paths.

OUR HOME

The Temple of ECK has been built in Chanhassen, Minnesota. Why? And what difference has it made to the whole movement of Eckankar?

I think any organization—religious, political, or social—needs a home. You need a home because you need a base to work from. But the Temple of ECK also provides a direct line of spiritual energy from the higher worlds that comes into the Physical Plane.

The Temple itself gives people an opportunity to find truth at their own level. The many ECK centers that are established around the world right now and the ECK temples that will come in different parts of the world are almost like different rooms in the same Temple. It's all under the teaching of the Mahanta, the Living ECK Master—the same teacher.

It's important to have spiritual learning centers around the world for people who don't have the inner connection, yet want to get divine truth. They will have the opportunity to go to one of these ECK centers or ECK temples that will be around the world and sing HU with others and also study the spiritual discourse lessons I provide for the members of ECK.

The Temple itself gives people an opportunity to find truth at their own level.

ARE THE ECK MASTERS REAL?

Much is written in Eckankar about the ECK Masters, the Order of the Vairagi Adepts. Are these archetypal images or real beings?

These are real beings. There are people who have come into Eckankar who have had experiences with people like Rebazar Tarzs years before they knew about the ECK Masters or became members of Eckankar. Or they've had experiences with Yaubl Sacabi and Fubbi Quantz. These ECK Masters served at the height of civilization throughout our current history and even earlier.

The ECK Masters have great compassion. They give love and mercy to the people they meet. All they want to do is pass along the gifts of God, but people have to earn them.

The ECK Masters have great compassion. They give love and mercy to the people they meet.

Is the Vairagi Order, of which you are the present leader, connected to any other brotherhood? If not, do you still work with other masters and teachers?

It's an independent spiritual order. But we work with the masters of the other orders because among the true leaders of any spiritual teaching—where people are truly interested in the spiritual welfare of the human race—there aren't any walls.

Each of these groups of spiritual adepts knows that it has a particular function to carry out. Each group has its own mission to God. There is no conflict. They allow people to go to whichever group they need for their own spiritual unfoldment.

HIGHEST REGIONS

Eckankar states that it can lead one to the highest regions on the inner planes. Can this also be achieved on other paths?

Each path has a particular purpose as far as bringing a person to a certain level. And it isn't always the highest teaching within that path that comes forward to the people. The lower order of teachings in each group might say, "This is the highest path."

You have to remember that these worlds that God set up are negative in nature so that Soul may develop Its spiritual qualities. The pattern for spiritual growth is set up so that people learn more by the lessons they gain through hardship. Not through things they learn when life is easy.

I'm afraid we're all like that here. We enjoy life when it's easy, but that's not necessarily when we learn our greatest spiritual lessons. We learn our best lessons when times are hard.

LEVELS OF CONSCIOUSNESS

Other religions group together cosmic consciousness and God-Realization as the same experience. Eckankar states that there is, in fact, a difference. How can we tell them apart?

Cosmic consciousness is directly connected with the Mental Plane. It comes from the mental region where all our thought, philosophy, logic, and various arts along this line come from. Cosmic consciousness is the high part of the mental region, and it gives primarily the Light of God but not the Sound.

Someone who had the experience of cosmic consciousness came to me to ask if this was God Consciousness. I didn't answer the person, because I can't. If someone has to ask, it isn't.

If you have God Consciousness, you don't have to tell anyone, outside of my role because it's my duty to do so. It's the duty of the spiritual leader of the teachings of ECK to announce himself and make the path of spiritual wisdom freely available to other people. So all those who are ready can find their way to it, so that I can help them put all their attention and efforts toward rising to a higher plane of existence than the physical.

The pattern for spiritual growth is set up so that people learn more by the lessons they gain through hardship.

PROVING THE PATH

What would you recommend a person do to prove the authenticity of this path?

I would suggest singing the word *HU*. If you are going to have any success on this path at all, generally you'll get it by singing HU. The way to sing HU is in a very long, drawn-out breath. Sing the word simply as HU-U-U-U-U.

If you are going to have any success on this path at all, generally you'll get it by singing HU.

Sing this song either silently or softly in prayer or meditation sessions for ten or fifteen minutes a day for a month. Try it this way. Then if nothing happens, give yourself a rest for a month or two. Later, if you remember, do it again. If nothing happens then, don't worry about it, because when the seeker is ready the Master appears. It's spiritual law.

When you're ready, you're going to find your next step on the spiritual path.

FUTURE OF ECKANKAR

What do you see is the future of this teaching?

Someday the teachings of ECK will be a major world religion. But it's not a foregone conclusion. It's going to take a lot of work by a lot of good people to make this happen.

DREAM TEACHINGS

How do the dream teachings of Eckankar differ from other dream teachings?

Dream teachings range from the silly to the highly mental. All can help a person to some degree, depending upon where that person is. The dream teachings of ECK follow the basic pattern of all the ECK teachings: they are grounded both in the physical teaching as well as the spiritual, the inner, subtle side. So a person who wants to learn how to dream the ECK way can study some of the ECK discourses as a part of membership.

In other words, you can become a member of ECK and study the ECK dream discourses. Or you may just read one of the ECK books. This is the outer dream, the first step or outer link that occurs to help you make the inner connection to actually having these dreams and understanding how these dreams work.

WHAT IS SOUL TRAVEL?

Why is there such a focus on Soul Travel? What is it?

Soul Travel also has its range of experience. Some people notice it as just a shift in consciousness. All of a sudden, something happens in their lives where they become aware that they understand something they haven't before. It comes in like a soft, golden kiss of God. Then, they just *know* something.

Soul Travel can also be a stronger experience where people are actually lifted completely out of the body and they have some experience in the other worlds. It depends on what they're ready for, what's necessary for their spiritual unfoldment.

Soul Travel deals exclusively with the expansion of spiritual awareness.

Why is it so important in Eckankar to learn Soul Travel?

Soul Travel, in its broader sense, is very important because it deals exclusively with the expansion of spiritual awareness. In other words, people have to, at some time, become aware of who and what they are. This knowledge is also opened to them through

dreams, or through some other way—their past lives
and the possibilities for the future.

But more important: Soul Travel—which means
moving into the higher regions of God, to regions
people haven't even been to before—opens them to
divine love.

This is more important than any of the other
journeys into inner space or anything of that nature.
Moving into the inner planes through Soul Travel—
whether in a very focused or a broad, expansive
manner—opens the heart to divine love. This is what
life is all about.

*The greatest
obstacle to God
is usually the
person himself.*

OVERCOMING OBSTACLES

*What would you say is the greatest obstacle for
someone trying to get to God-Realization?*

The greatest obstacle to God is usually the person
himself. People, in their experience in life, go through
all the ups and downs of everyday living. They get
the feeling that they learn something, but so often,
in a single lifetime, people don't learn a whole lot.
This is why there is such a need to experience going
through many, many lives.

By the time they come to the lifetime where they
find ECK, they've had just about every experience
you can imagine. Unless it happens to be one of their
first lifetimes in ECK. Then people generally leave
the path in disappointment and disillusionment, only
to come back centuries later.

*So what is the key for learning to step aside and
not get in the way?*

Putting your attention so much on God through
singing HU or some other method that God becomes

the substance of your life.

When I say this, I do it with some hesitation. When I say, "God becomes the substance of your life," people put together all the wrong messages ever gathered in this life or in previous lives. They put it together all wrong. For instance they say, "All right, to love God a lot means to leave my family. It means to go out in the desert somewhere, to go up in the mountains, and cut myself off from humanity. That is showing my love for God." Nothing could be farther from the truth.

That is why I'm really hesitant about saying that God must become the entire focus of the person's life. What I would suggest instead is to sing HU or some other name of God. It will lift you into the higher levels of spiritual realization.

Sing HU or some other name of God. It will lift you into the higher levels of spiritual realization.

FRIDAY FAST

Can you speak about the Friday fast in Eckankar? For instance, is it OK to have vegetables instead of fruits for the Friday fast?

Yes. In the early days of Eckankar there was more emphasis on a twenty-four-hour water fast on Fridays as the primary fast. I discourage that today. Unless it's done under a physician's care, people can hurt themselves. They destroy their muscles. Some actually go very much out of balance.

I usually suggest that on Friday, instead of doing any austerities with food, simply put your attention on God or the Mahanta, the Inner Master. Put your attention there as much as you can throughout the twenty-four hours of a Friday. This will help you spiritually more than any of the other things you've tried, and it's a lot kinder to you.

It'll keep you more in balance so that you can enjoy living. So many people have the misunderstanding that living the spiritual life means to cut yourself off from family and friends or do things that cause all kinds of unnecessary problems. All we do then is create more karma for ourselves. It's such a shame.

I just try to show people how to become responsible human beings who are good to their families and helpful to their neighbors.

I try to show people how to become responsible human beings who are good to their families and helpful to their neighbors.

IN ONE LIFETIME

Can we actually rid ourselves of all past-life karma and not have to reincarnate again? Is it really possible to achieve this in one lifetime?

Yes, if the person keeps his face toward the Light of God and listens to the Sound.

Many people who get on the path of God are basically from the frozen-food society. They want to do it for about five to ten minutes a day for five or ten days. Then they lose interest. They wonder, *Why didn't this work for me?* They give their life over to something that is going to change them forever, and if in five or ten days nothing happens, they get so disillusioned that they give up the path to God. Then they say it doesn't work.

That's sometimes the nature of the person who hasn't lived in the lower worlds very long and hasn't many past lives to his or her credit.

It's difficult in my role as the spiritual leader. There are just a few people who can really recognize the gift of the Inner and Outer Master. Those who can, accept it. Those who can't, reject it.

The people who reject it are usually those who criticize and make fun of the spiritual leader because they don't know better. But the spiritual leader never holds it against them. He was that way too once. It's just part of the human condition.

SOUL'S DANCE

I had a lucid dream where I was dancing through the ethers with thousands of Souls, all being drawn to a central point. I was full of joy, knowing that no matter what we do in this world, we are always going to be drawn back to this central point.

A very spiritual dream. It's the dance of Soul for God. The joy is in meeting the true Master and having the true love of God.

I have seen people come to an Eckankar seminar and begin crying for no reason. Inwardly, as Soul, they have heard the Voice of God. And God has said, "I love you because you are a part of me, and I am calling you home."

It's a personal experience so strong that it changes that person's life. At that point he is no longer the same. Few of his friends and acquaintances can understand what major turning point occurred to him at that moment. It's just beyond words. But it is life changing.

Sometimes the love is so strong, it's really incredible. It fills you with joy. It cleanses the heart, it purifies it, and it gives the person a readiness to accept more of God's love.

This is the secret of the inner teachings.

Love cleanses the heart, it purifies it, and it gives the person a readiness to accept more of God's love.

Interview, The Golden Age, *Sydney, Australia, November 27, 1993*

You have to ask God, "Show me thy ways; show me thy truth; show me thy love." And then listen.

5

FROM DARKNESS
TO LIGHT

*I*t always strikes me funny when we are
translating a talk for a number of different languages. I'll say something, and
those in the audience who understand English will applaud. Then the people who get the fast-
est translation—maybe the Spanish—will applaud
next. They get a quick translation because they can
say things more quickly. Finally, at the very end, after everyone else has applauded, the Germans do.

I can say this because my background is German.
My parents spoke German. In German, you put a
sentence together with a lot of phrases, then at the
very end comes the verb. It takes a very superior
mind to keep track of a German sentence.

This is one of the achievements of the German
people—to be able to speak their language.

TWO ASPECTS

Every time one of these talks comes up, I find it
difficult to explain the precepts of God and Its two
aspects, the Light and Sound. After you've heard
about them for a while as an ECKist, you learn to
see and hear the truth of the words of ECK.

But it takes a while. It takes experiences in the dream state. And some of you have experiences with Soul Travel.

As you have these experiences, you understand there is more to life than you realized. And so you have a greater understanding of the way things are. In a way you leave behind your friends and acquaintances who haven't received your understanding of how truth works and what truth is.

GOD'S VOICE

Someone asked me this afternoon, "What are the Light and Sound of God?" I've explained this so many different times, in so many ways.

What kind of word does God speak? "I love you, therefore you exist."

Basically it comes down to this: The Light and Sound of God together are the Voice of God. In scriptures we know It as the Word or Logos. In other words, it's God speaking from beyond creation to Its creation.

And what kind of word does God speak? Is it always in the human tongue, something you can understand like "Thou shalt not"? Is this what the God of love is really concerned about?

It is more along the lines of "I love you, therefore you exist." This is the greatest commandment of all, because it's the commandment of love.

LOVE AND KARMA

Of course, people in the human consciousness do not understand divine love. The human experience throughout all the many lives you have had is about trying to understand love in all its forms, from the most perverse—the lowest form—all the way to the highest form.

There are penalties that go along with practicing each one of these different forms of love, from the lowest in your earliest lifetime to the higher forms you grow into as you go farther along the path to God.

The penalty, or price to pay, occurs because of karma.

Karma is simply cause and effect: If you do something that hurts another person, you're going to have to pay for it. It's that simple.

And there's something beside bad karma, which I've just given an example of. Doing something that hurts someone and having to pay for it is bad karma. On the other hand, if you do something that's good, you will get a reward for it. The balance, the accounting of it all, goes into your book of records, into a Causal record, an Akashic record.

This is the total accounting of how you stand with karma in your life today. Your karmic balance sheet affects how satisfied you are with yourself and your spiritual unfoldment. In other words, are you happy or unhappy with life?

Karma is simply cause and effect: If you do something that hurts another person, you're going to have to pay for it.

VIEWPOINTS ABOUT GOD

There are people who believe in God and those who don't, and there are people who simply don't know whether or not God exists. When I say this, I'm speaking of God in the sense that most of us in our society are used to thinking: that God is a personal God, like a snowy-bearded grandpa who always treats us kindly, speaks nicely to us, and hardly ever uses a harsh voice. And if we think of God as a grandpa with a long white beard, we're going to have a hard time with someone who doesn't see God this way.

Other people in other societies believe in God as

an impersonal being. So right away people from one culture will have a hard time communicating with those who believe in God differently.

Those who believe in the kindly grandpa are going to have a hard time with the idea that God is an impersonal force, a creative element that created the lower worlds and everything that exists in them. It's very different. It's another way of looking at creation. And who's to say if it's right or wrong?

So in each society you'll have people who believe in God, people who don't believe in God, and people who don't know if they believe in God.

In some societies it isn't even important whether or not someone believes in God. It's more important to these people to simply live life and treat their neighbors and family with love and respect. Those are the values of certain societies in a particular period of history.

Each religion, each belief is just a splinter of the whole truth about God and the existence of God.

Each religion, each belief is just a splinter of the whole truth about God and the existence of God. Perhaps God is a lot bigger than anything our little mind can wrap its arms around.

This comes as a shock to some people. They feel the God they believe in wraps His arms around all creation, when in fact it is the believer that wraps the arms of his own mind around this being and calls it God.

He gives this being powers to go forth and create everything in this world. In other words, God then becomes a creation of man's own mind. But if you ever told people this, they would become very upset with you. They'd think anyone who believed in your sort of God was probably possessed by Satan.

The best thing to do at this point would be to get out of their society as quickly as possible.

UNDERSTANDING THE NATURE OF TRUTH

The human mind becomes frustrated with something that is greater than its own self. When something greater than the human mind exists, it threatens the human mind. If people are totally caught up in the powers of the human mind, they're going to have a very hard time accepting the existence of God.

I find that the people who have the best relationship with life and understand the spiritual realities and God more clearly than the average person—no matter their financial situation, rich or poor—are generally able to be happy with themselves and others.

People who are miserable, constantly complaining, making problems for others, and saying others have abused them—they can go on and on—these people usually don't understand the nature of truth or the nature of God.

YOUR OWN CREATION

Today you are simply living out your own creation.

I know this is a harsh thing to say, but it's so. Because if you're in harmony with the spiritual principles at all, you're going to know that the life you have is the one you have created for yourself in some way, at some time. Today you are simply living out your own creation.

This isn't to say you have created yourself. God created you. But it's what you have done with your mind and your beliefs. It usually becomes very self-centered. A part of the mind thinks very highly of itself. It's the nature of the mind to do this. When it thinks this way, it feels it is all-powerful; it feels that it understands creation in some way, even though the person would have to admit it is just a theory.

The person says, "I know it's only a theory, but my belief about God is better than yours. I can't prove mine, but I don't like yours."

It's this kind of illogic that you sometimes hear from people of a very strong mind who have a very strong belief in the Divinity. They grant no freedom or space to anyone or any belief other than their own.

From Darkness into Light

If you're in ECK, you probably wouldn't want to be part of such a belief system. And you'll find that many of the people in ECK have come from just about every religion on earth.

We have people from all over, from every religion, every philosophy. Some people have been in three, four, five, or six different ones because they desire truth, God, and divine love so sincerely.

When they found the answer was missing in one of the paths, they kept moving. They wanted to move from darkness into light.

How Most People Pray

So many people tell God what to do. But if they would just listen to God sometimes, they would find it an enlightening experience.

Somehow over the centuries, people have gotten into the very bad habit of dictating to God, like an employee. And if God doesn't hear it the first time, they repeat it. Then they throw a little tantrum, cry, and get angry. People don't realize this is the attitude behind their prayers when they're telling God what to do.

Maybe a person is a spendthrift. They spend money like there's no tomorrow. When the money's there it goes to the ponies, for gambling, to the state lotteries, to the bottle. They pray to God, "I want to have money. I don't feel I should be poor like this.

So many people tell God what to do. But if they would just listen to God sometimes, they would find it an enlightening experience.

I deserve a better life. I'm your humble servant."

Then they bow down really low, into the dirt, striking what they think is the proper pose—as if God's going to be fooled.

And life goes on pretty much the same as before. The person keeps praying as hard as ever and keeps wasting money and resources the same as ever.

Transfer to the Next Life

Then the end of this life comes, and the person goes into the other worlds. He finds he has to come back to earth, that it wasn't just a one-way trip to heaven.

He's disappointed. He says, "You mean I'm really going to have to learn how to get it right, how to live a life of balance?" And the Lords of Karma say, "Yep. For sure."

Most people who die go to the Astral Plane before transferring back for another life. Sometimes they go to the Causal Plane or the Mental Plane, but mostly they go to the Astral. As soon as they leave the body they realize they haven't done a whole lot of good with the life they just completed.

The Lords of Karma are very impersonal about the whole thing. "Here's your balance sheet; look it over," they say.

There are usually a lot of minuses: Did not unfold spiritually. Did not discipline myself to get along with what I have. Treated others poorly. Cheated my employer (because he owes me more than I make). This sort of thing.

Very few people remember their past lives, especially past the age of six.

Children Remember Past Lives

Then they come back into the next life with hardly a memory of what they've been in the past.

Very few people remember their past lives, especially past the age of six.

Children up to the age of four generally remember one, two, or three of their lifetimes, but the parents don't believe them. They don't believe in past lives, especially if they're Christian. They tell the children, "You have some imagination" or "Stop talking foolishness, and do your homework."

Reincarnation is one of the basic principles of life.

They don't have the ears to hear truth as their children speak it. And after age five or six, the children begin to go through society's schooling system, and the window on past lives gets shut.

Then the children grow up, become parents, and don't understand their own children.

Reincarnation is one of the basic principles of life. Another one is karma, cause and effect—that if you do something to another, whether good or bad, you're going to get the effect of it.

This goes on and on until you become very experienced in the laws of life. And as you become experienced in the laws of life, you realize there must be something more than merely existing as a human being. Until you realize the truths of the Light and Sound of God, you never really understand there's more to life than just existing.

If you look back to how you were before ECK, to a large degree life was just existing. By this I mean wondering what it's all about, what it all means, why are you here.

PROVING THE EXISTENCE OF GOD

An agnostic joined Eckankar. He stayed an agnostic for a long time, but he developed a great respect for life.

He used to love to go fishing. He's from the midwestern United States, and he'd go out to the western part of Colorado to do his trout fishing.

This man used a special hook that had no barbs so that he could unhook the fish with the smallest amount of injury and throw the fish back into the stream. He'd thank the fish, the way the Native Americans used to. They always gave thanks for any food that they needed to take from the theater of life because they realized that to survive one must eat another, whether it's animal or plant. It's a part of living.

Today we have people who are very self-righteous about being vegetarians. They feel they are more righteous because they don't eat meat. They are eating plants, as if plants don't have life or consciousness.

It's an attitude that says, "I am better than you because I'm a vegetarian."

I have to say, "Oops, you just slid right back to where you started."

Self-righteousness is a very heavy anchor to drag around in life—whether it's because of your belief system, your religion, or your dietary practice. Whatever you eat, it's important to give thanks for what you take and not waste it.

Whatever you eat, it's important to give thanks for what you take and not waste it.

This is the nature of life, and it's especially important as more of us crowd onto this little planet, polluting it in every way.

May the Blessings Be

This man went up into the mountains of Colorado. He was an agnostic, but he gave thanks. He appreciated life. But he still didn't know whether there was a God, and he wanted proof about God's existence.

He was walking along the edge of a stream to a spot where he thought the fishing would be better. Suddenly he saw a very large trout. The trout looked sick; it had a fungus on its head. The man knew the fish wasn't going to last much longer. A great deal of compassion flowed from his heart to the fish. He gave the blessing of the Vairagi Adepts, the ECK Masters who are given the duty of bringing the message of truth, of Light and Sound, to the people of earth who are ready for it.

The man said, "May the blessings be."

Not "I hope you get better, fish," or "God, please make this fish better" or something like this. We don't tell God what to do. God has enough things to do without our help—actually God has more things to do because of our help!

Suddenly inside the fisherman's heart, love began to grow. He had opened his heart by the simple blessing, and this divine love began to flow through him to the fish. And as the love of God came into the heart of the fisherman, he knelt beside the stream, and the fish swam up close to him. The love just grew and grew.

The fisherman wanted to reach down and rub the stomach of this fish. Then he thought, *No, it'll break the magic of the moment.* And as he thought this, his heart center began to close again. The love began to diminish, and the trout swam away.

This is an example of how sometimes God's love enters the human heart. It doesn't necessarily happen in a cathedral—that may be the last place it happens, because a cathedral is a creation of man's mind. There's a rightful place for temples, a place to come together and sing the holy name of God and study God's word. We have a Temple of ECK, and there will be more of them. But there is also a time to go inside in silence, to a quiet place, and just listen to the Voice of God. This is what you do in contemplation, in your fifteen to twenty minutes a day. You listen for the Voice of God and watch for some appearance of the Light of God.

When the Light and Sound come into the inner vision, the Spiritual Eye, or the heart, you'll be filled with a joy and love you've never felt before.

GATES OF HEAVEN

I met with someone today, and the love of Divine Spirit began to come into his heart. It quite surprised him, caught him off guard. Tears began to run down his face.

He was almost embarrassed by it because he didn't expect his heart to open and divine love to pour through. He didn't know what to do, what to make of it. It wasn't something that happened often to him.

The same thing has happened to me; it happens to other people. It can come at any time, under any condition or circumstance.

But it only comes at your invitation. In other words, you have to ask God, "Show me thy ways; show me truth; show me thy love." And then listen. If you go on banging on the doors of heaven with your little fists, no one will hear.

No one will open the doors, because that's not how the doorbell to the gates of heaven works. The gates open from the inside outward, but only when you have made all the spiritual preparations to walk through. Heaven is the place where divine love is kept and where divine love flows. It's the heart of God.

And when you qualify through your love for God,

When the Light and Sound come into the inner vision, the Spiritual Eye, or the heart, you'll be filled with a joy and love you've never felt before.

Heaven is the place where divine love is kept and where divine love flows. It's the heart of God.

the gates will open up to you. You will become a different person.

FALLING INTO KARMA

Often the only analogy I can make to the love of God is in a poor human way. Many people get married because that's the way of life. They fall in love, and they fall into karma.

Two people recognize each other from their mutual past, and they have something to work out. There is a very strong attraction between them. So they work out their karma through the ways society has approved of: marriage or a relationship or something like that.

When two people fall in love, I see two Souls on the journey to truth unconsciously doing what they need to do to balance their own books of life, to balance the scales with each other. Sometime in the past, their balance sheets became full of either too many pluses or too many minuses. They've got to get together to balance the books just a little bit.

As they get together, each couple takes on the entire karmic background of the other person's family, if you can imagine. Not quite as strongly as the person himself or herself, but in varying degrees, depending on the closeness of the family to the couple that has become one through the marriage union.

The people may continue their entire life without having ever known the true meaning of love, although they think they know what it is.

This relationship of falling in love or falling into karma goes on. Then at some point, things change.

There are the rare cases where two people come together with a higher form of love than this karmic bond. When they have this higher form of love, they live for each other because they live for God and they live for life. They live with humility, with the spirit of service which says, "What can I do for you?"

People with the highest form of love are always serving each other without ever — or very seldom — saying, "Why do I always have to pick up your laundry off the floor, just so you can throw it down again?" This is earth, after all. But basically what exists between them is love. Everything they do in their relationship, the way they split up the chores or whatever, is built upon love. It's entirely different from a relationship built purely on karma. If you've had the ordinary relationship and then you find love, you will recognize those few other people on earth who also know the meaning of love.

There aren't that many. Most of the people think they are searching for truth when they are really searching for love.

A RECIPE FOR LOVE

Even a couple who hasn't had true love before can find it. How do you do it? You can't take so many cups of this and that ingredient and put it together to bake for thirty-five minutes at so many degrees to get love. It doesn't quite work that easily.

I can give you hints. I can provide the recipe book and point out a recipe, like recommending a really good bread recipe from a bread cookbook. I can even find you the ingredients, set everything out, get the baking pans ready, and heat the oven.

But unless a person has the sense or discipline to take what's there and put the parts together in the right way, the result isn't going to turn out. The bread won't be as good.

People with the highest form of love are always serving each other.

Most people think they are searching for truth when they are really searching for love.

Same recipe, same ingredients—but two different cooks. And you can't make someone a cook just by giving them a cookbook.

Reader's Digest ran a little story about a new cook who wanted to double a recipe. It called for 1/4 cup of oil, so he used 1/2 cup. He doubled all the other ingredients too.

Then he doubled the baking time. From that moment on, he lost the recipe.

SPIRITUAL ROLE MODELS

Cats need a lot of freedom. Dogs do too, but they don't know it. Cats know it, and they demand it. If you don't give it to them, they are very unhappy creatures.

When you return from a trip, cats will let you know if you've mistreated them by not giving them the proper kennel or place to stay while you were gone. They may let you pet them; they may not. With a dog it's different: When you get back from vacation, the dog comes running up to you, tongue hanging out.

The dog says, "So glad to see you, so glad to see you. Glad you're back. Let's go home."

A cat says, "So. Where've you been? Had a good time?"

Then the cat doesn't come out of the cage. It says, "Look at this crummy place you've kept me. I hope you had a good time, but you never think of anybody else. I think I'm going to stay in here and die."

The owner has to reach in, grab the cat, and pull it out to take it home. The cat allows this without too much scratching because the cat really does want to go home.

I don't think a dog has opinions. A dog has love.

A dog, I think, is generations and lifetimes ahead of a cat as far as divine love goes.

Cats are self-centered, have opinions, and like things a certain way. They like to run the household. Dogs are more like what we work toward in ECK. One day people will become Co-workers with God after they have had all the experience. Dogs are there already. Dogs are co-workers.

They say, "What can I do for you? Bring your slippers? You don't want the paper, I'll get it anyway."

Spiritually if you want to have a role model and don't want to look to other people or a Master, look to dogs. Dogs have a good relationship with life, generally.

THE CRYING CAT

A woman kept a kennel for cats as a sideline. People who were going on vacation brought their cats, and she took care of them. She loved cats and had a very big kennel for them. She also built very big cages for the cats. Her business card had a motto like "We love cats" or "Love is everything."

The kennel gave the cats a lot of space and a lot of freedom. Because of this, she couldn't keep as many cats as other kennels, so her business wasn't as profitable as it could've been, but if you love something very much it's not always profitable. Most of the cats who stayed with her really liked being there.

The cats were happy; they were happy to go home when their owners came back or they would have been happy to stay. Life was pretty good for the cats.

They became pretty much like dogs in that respect. When an owner would come to pick up a cat, the cat would say, "Happy to see you; you're back, very nice. You took good care of me. Like the cages here;

One day people will become Co-workers with God after they have had all the experience. Dogs are there already.

like the company."

Except for this one cat named Busy. Busy was a good cat. But whenever the kennel owner would walk out of the room, Busy began to cry.

Cats can really make a racket if they decide to cry, like some people crying to God. An awful racket. No one else could stand it. Busy cried and cried and cried. Whenever the woman who owned the kennel left the room, the cat would begin wailing.

By about the fifth day, her roommates were going crazy with the noise. They'd go out to eat just to have some peace and quiet. Everyone was losing their sanity, and they didn't have much love left.

The kennel owner had set up this whole little community that existed because of love. But then there was warfare.

It was just like God putting a bunch of Souls on earth and saying, "Now you exist because I love you." Then what happens? There are centuries of warfare and cutting each other with words and knives. God gives people just enough creativity to create gunpowder, and then it gets worse. He gives them more creativity, and they split the atom and things get even worse.

Then the kennel owner began to be very angry at Busy, which was a surprise because the woman was usually so full of love. But the crying cat was destroying the love and harmony that had been in the kennel.

When she finally reached bottom, she turned the situation over to the Mahanta, the Inner Master in ECK, the inner side of myself. She said, "Mahanta, I can't do anything. If you or any of the other ECK Masters can help, please do something. The cat's driving me out of my mind."

A Special Dream

That night, the kennel owner had a dream. In her dream she saw Prajapati, the ECK Master who takes a special interest in animals. Prajapati came up to Busy, picked the cat up, and began petting it.

As he petted the cat, a golden heart appeared on Busy's chest. Busy loved the attention and quieted down.

This all happened in the inner planes, the dream state. The inner worlds are as real as this outer physical world. There's a connection between the two. Sometimes if things aren't working out right out here, instead of going through years of karma and trouble you can get things back on track if you know how to go to the inner worlds. You sing the love song to God, HU, and the Mahanta will take you to the other worlds. He'll give you an experience where you either gain the insight to change conditions or improve yourself. Sometimes this is all that's required to make things work better in the physical world.

Soon other ECK Masters appeared in the woman's dream. Busy was happily running back and forth from one ECK Master to another, enjoying all the attention and petting.

Rebazar Tarzs, an ECK Master who used to serve in Tibet, picked Busy up and said, "Busy, let's go for a little walk." And Rebazar took the cat to a dark cave that was nearby.

When they came to the entrance, the Master said, "Busy, this is a cave, and we're going to go inside. It's very important for you to see and understand what this cave means to you." They walked inside and saw a deep pit. Rebazar explained that the cat had walked into a pit on the physical plane in a previous life, fell into it, and cried to get out.

The inner worlds are as real as this outer physical world.

No one could hear its cries deep in the cave. So the cat perished. This terror had stayed with the cat into this present life.

All of us have lived before.

EXPLORING THE SOURCE OF FEAR

All of us have lived before. You've had some very good experiences and some very bad experiences. When you come into this life, certain of those experiences are going to be highlighted for you because this is what you need to work out.

This is why very young children have nightmares. They're remembering past lives.

Sometimes the individual met a terrifying death or torture, either rightfully or wrongfully earned. It was a part of that life experience, and the memory comes back as nightmares and night terrors.

This also happened to Busy the cat. It had a fear of being left alone in a dark place by itself. So Rebazar explained it to the cat, and the golden heart on Busy's chest began to shine, casting light around them.

"How would you like to explore the cave?" Rebazar asked the cat. In other words, explore the source of your fear.

And of course Busy became like an ordinary cat, very inquisitive. They walked through the cave, and the Light of God came through the golden heart and lit up the pitfalls, holes, and other dangers.

The ECKist saw what happened to the cat on the inner planes. And from that time on, Busy never had the crying problem again.

Love Drives Out Fear

Truth reveals itself through the Light and Sound of God. Whether it comes to an animal, to you, or to someone else, it fills your heart with love. And when your heart is full of love, what room is there for fear?

Love drives out fear. When people are born into this lower physical existence, their hearts are open. But in the experiences they go through to become more godlike, in the lifetimes of hardships, the heart closes down. The golden heart closes, and the Light of God disappears.

But those of you who love truth and wisdom are somewhere, sometime going to make the effort to open your heart again. Because you realize something is missing. You're not your full self.

You're not living the full life that you, as a spiritual being, should lead.

From darkness to light is Soul's journey in the lower worlds. This is a world of darkness, and Soul wants to return to the source of Its being, which is light. Soul is light, a spark of God.

And when your heart is full of love, what room is there for fear?

Soul is light, a spark of God.

ECK South Pacific Seminar, Sydney, Australia, Saturday, November 27, 1993

She realized that this one experience in the delicatessen was a turning point in her life because someone had bothered to give her the gift of love through simply looking directly into her eyes.

6

THE LESSONS OF LOVE AND THANKS

Someone was kind enough to give me photographs of the seminar that took place here ten years ago. The film from ten years ago was a lot better than the film we have today; it captured the essence of youth better than film does today.

So I do appreciate the gift of these photographs because you don't find film like that anymore.

My eyes aren't what they used to be either. I went to the eye doctor, trying to get some contact lenses I could work with. It took ten months. Before that I had spent five years trying to get the correct lenses, but my eyes kept changing. You get to middle age and beyond middle age, and the eye doctor has a hard time catching up, keeping up, and finally getting ahead to get you a prescription that works.

I asked my eye doctor for special contact lenses where I could see well at a distance but also at reading range—without holding my notes down by my toes. Otherwise I have to wear glasses.

My talks are often videotaped, and nothing dates a talk more quickly than the changing styles of clothing or eyeglasses. I find it convenient to wear simple suits and contact lenses instead of glasses, because those styles change every few years. Dated videos feel wrong, like you're watching something from the twilight zone. You feel out of touch watching it, so I try to make things simple.

GIVING FROM YOUR HEART

If you give from your heart, this is the most valuable gift you can give anyone.

This is the Year of Giving. When I announced the title of the spiritual year at the ECK Worldwide Seminar in Los Angeles, some of the ECK initiates were upset that it was the Year of Giving. They thought it was all about money. But this isn't my intention.

Giving money at any time is important, of course, because in this world it makes things go. But I think there are so many more important ways of giving.

If you give from your heart, this is the most valuable gift you can give anyone.

TALK-SHOW HOST

I've been clearing my throat a lot. I have to watch what I eat very carefully; I've mentioned this before. It's interesting. Back in the States, I listen to a certain talk-show host. Every once in a while he gets a bad cold. Then he's off his radio show for a few days.

He doesn't realize that the reason he loses his voice is because of his diet.

He likes to eat, he tells people what he eats, and he's quite a large man. But sometimes it causes him problems. I'm always wondering if I should send him a letter and say, "You know, you've got to watch what you eat if you want to do your show every day."

LESSONS OF LOVE AND THANKS

Sometimes the lessons in life are so difficult. This is a world of lessons—your lessons, the lessons of your family, my lessons, everyone else's lessons. They're lessons of love and thanks.

When we go through the experiences that are part of our everyday lives, often there are times of joy in between the lessons. But sometimes it seems there are a lot more rocks in our way than soft grass to walk on. There are always things underfoot, things to make us trip or stumble.

But these stumbling blocks can be stepping-stones, as I've mentioned before. It depends on our attitude.

If someone recognizes and appreciates life and its lessons, if they realize that these things in life that appear as difficulties are really gifts of God to make us stronger spiritually, it helps. It may not seem like help when we lose a loved one or something like that. But our viewpoint can help us recover sooner. It can help us realize that in ECK we know that Soul is eternal, in the true sense. To me, eternal means without beginning or ending.

Soul is without beginning or ending.

God created Soul outside the parameters of time and space. Soul is without beginning or ending.

Some people believe that Soul comes into existence at the birth of the infant, but this is not quite an accurate belief. If it were, then Soul would not be eternal, because Soul would have a beginning in this finite world. But Soul has existed before the birth of the child.

A HEALING LIGHT

A chela named Linda grew up Episcopalian, in the religion of her family. In grade school, she got into Christian Science; in her teen years she came into contact with the Unity teachings.

Then she found out about meditation. Since then

she has found Eckankar and become an ECKist. But in the years before ECK, when she was a teenager practicing meditation, someone told her how to work with pictures, to see things as pictures in the Spiritual Eye.

So one day she sat down to do this, and right away she had an experience. She saw a beautiful and pure yellow light, like the most beautiful lemon pie you can imagine.

This was the Light of God, one of the two aspects of the Holy Spirit. The other is the Sound.

When Linda saw this yellow light, it was so beautiful that it healed and uplifted her.

When Linda saw this yellow light, it was so beautiful that it healed and uplifted her. She became a part of the light and went into the light. Then after some time—she couldn't remember exactly what had happened—she came back into her body.

"This meditation's OK," she said.

The next day she tried the very same technique again, but she saw nothing except absolute blackness. Worse, she started pushing. She stared into her Spiritual Eye, which is that point right above and between the eyebrows.

And she began to see faces coming out of the blackness, staring back at her. Linda didn't know what these faces were.

Sometimes they were faces she had worn in previous lives. It was as if she were looking at a reflection of herself in a shiny mirror or a pool. Other times they were faces of people who were close to her, with whom she had a karmic tie and a karmic burden. People who would play a part in her life in the future as they had already played a part in the past. The faces frightened her. So after a few more tries to contact the light again, she gave up.

But this was the beginning of her experience with

the Light and Sound of God.

Two years later, Linda married and moved to another part of the United States. Her husband turned out to be a very brutish man. He beat her; she always had black eyes. He was constantly threatening to take her life. Sometimes he bragged that he had taken other people's lives. She never knew if he was telling the truth about having hurt these other people; she just knew there were a lot of people in that area who had turned up missing.

A DREAM OF PROTECTION

About this time, Linda began having dreams that said, "Move. Move away from here to save your life."

But her self-esteem was low, and her spirit was broken. She figured, *What's the difference if my husband takes my life?* But the dreams kept persisting.

One day, she finally said inwardly, "Show me. Is there some reason I should live?"And a special dream came to her. It showed her future possibilities where she had a family, children, and a happier life. This convinced her to get on a bus and go back to California, where she had grown up.

After her divorce she remarried, then became pregnant with her first child. The dreams had taken her safely out of a very dangerous situation.

Through the dreams and her inner knowingness, she realized that her ex-husband had indeed had the intention of taking her life and burying her in the woods. That would have been the end of her.

TRIP TO THE CAUSAL PLANE

About this time, one of her childhood friends, Georgie, died suddenly in a car accident. This was a real shock to Linda because she'd never lost anyone close to her before.

To her, death meant the end of existence. And the idea that Georgie no longer existed was something Linda couldn't quite deal with. She fell into a deep despondency, crying a lot, trying to figure out what had happened to Georgie.

Then one night as she was lying in bed, she saw Georgie standing by her bed.

"Georgie, how are you doing?" Linda said.

"Fine," Georgie answered.

"But you're dead, you don't exist," she said.

"Well, as you can see, I'm here."

Linda looked at Georgie in awe. *He must know what it's like on the other side,* she realized. "I've always felt that death meant the end of existence," she told him. "But you are here."

"Yeah, if you want to see, come along. I'll show you," Georgie said.

"No, I've got to take care of my baby," Linda remembered. "I can't leave now."

"Don't worry," he said, "I can bring you back."And since Linda trusted her friend, she said, "OK."

Georgie took her into the Causal Plane, into an area where the Akashic records are stored, the seed place of all the karma of past lives.

Georgie took her into the Causal Plane, into an area where the Akashic records are stored, the seed place of all the karma of past lives. She saw these long chutes or slides, like farmers use in barn lofts for dropping hay to the cattle below. Souls, looking like adult human beings, were standing at the top of the slide. As they slid down, they kept changing form until they became infants. Then they'd plop down into the world, crying and wondering what had happened. It was a cold, dark world after the light of the Causal Plane.

THE SLIDE OF REINCARNATION

These Souls had been adults who had died on earth and gone to the Causal Plane to await their time of reincarnation. They'd get on this slide of reincarnation and go sliding right back into another body on earth. But the babies only had a small memory in the back of their minds of who and what they'd been in their previous lives.

Linda realized that the death of the physical body here on earth is not the death of the personality. The personality lives beyond the death of the human body.

We're not talking about Soul now, we're talking about the personality: the Astral, Causal, and Mental bodies of the individual. Not until Soul is reincarnated does the personality die. This is why so many times after a parent or a loved one dies, people have dream experiences with them.

Not until Soul is reincarnated does the personality die.

Why? They are seeing these people as the personality, or the complex that the personality stands for, meaning the Astral or Causal body.

At the base level, the physical body dies. People then take up residence on the Astral Plane. It's pretty much the same as here on earth, except they may take on a younger appearance. But the personality itself is extinguished when they go down the slide of reincarnation and come back to earth.

This explains why you see your loved ones or even pets in your dreams after they have passed on.

AKASHIC RECORDS

After Georgie showed Linda the slide, he said, "We're going to go a little farther now and see the Akashic records."

"Great!" said Linda. "I've always wanted to see my records."

"I can only show them to you for a brief moment," Georgie said.

"There's only one life I really want to see anyway," said Linda, "the one that deals with the life I'm in now."

Linda's past lives came out like a computer print-out, and the piece of paper was very long. It flowed out onto the floor. "Wow, you're one of those old ones," said Georgie. "You've been around a long time."

Linda very quickly took the opportunity to look at this life and find out why she had to go through certain experiences, why this life was so difficult for her. As soon as she'd finished, she said, "I'm satisfied now," and Georgie put the records away.

Georgie explained that his own printout of the Akashic records was very short; he'd had very few lifetimes on the physical plane. This is why it had been so difficult for him to learn. In school he had been classed as a slow learner, mildly retarded. It was difficult for him to pick up new things because he hadn't enough experiences about how things were done in the physical world.

Reincarnation clears up a lot of mysteries. This is why Eckankar has something to offer you.

CLEARING UP MYSTERIES

Many people don't understand that there is a reason for people being born either as geniuses or slow learners.

Some have been here many lifetimes. They have practiced as musicians, for example, for lifetimes before this one. They pick up their interest in music when they come back. People call them geniuses, and they think it's a big mystery how it's possible for Mozart to play the piano at age four.

Reincarnation clears up a lot of mysteries. This is why Eckankar has something to offer you. Not just because of the fact of reincarnation, which is part of our teachings; not just because of karma, which is cause and effect.

But because of something more than this: divine love.

GETTING OFF THE WHEEL OF KARMA

How do you get off the wheel of karma? How do you get to the point where you have enough experience? When you have enough experience, you're going to be ready for the path of ECK.

Maybe not for your whole life, but long enough to get the lessons, insight, and wisdom you need for the next stage of your spiritual journey. Some people go off to another teaching because of the demands of their spiritual unfoldment.

That's why when people come into Eckankar, I say, "Welcome. It's good to have you back." Most people don't know that they were here once before.

When they leave, I say, "Have a good trip. See you later. No hard feelings."

Because what's the difference? We're going to see each other again. That's the divine law. You're going to have to go through your lessons until the experiences of life give you the wisdom, love, and understanding that you need to someday take a step higher on the spiritual ladder and ultimately become a Co-worker with God.

This is the goal in ECK: to become a Co-worker with God.

This is the goal in ECK: to become a Co-worker with God.

BACK TO ECK

This is the reason I don't try to hold people when they want to go. When they go, they go. And when they come back, I let them come back.

Unless they've severely hurt someone spiritually by leaving ECK, unless they've taken other people off the path and picked up some of their karma— I let them come back. If they have created some very bad karma for themselves or caused others to pick up karma, then sometimes I don't let them back.

I tell them, "What's the difference? You might learn something in this lifetime so when you come back to ECK you'll appreciate it more."

But 90 percent of the time, I let them come back because they have learned something. They've gone on the fast track of life, and life has taught them something they couldn't get any other way. Who should begrudge them that?

I certainly won't, nor should you. There's no reason to hold on to anyone or anything. In the worlds of God, there's no way to become lost.

There's no way to miss out on the blessings of God unless you turn your back on the love and thanks that are yours as a gift.

LEARNING FROM TRUST

There's no way to miss out on the blessings of God unless you turn your back on the love and thanks that are yours as a gift. Linda had learned the love and thanks that come from trust in someone she had known as a friend.

Georgie was the kind of person she thought she'd like to marry someday. But Georgie never noticed her in that way; she was just a friend of his sister's. So Linda never got to marry Georgie, and then suddenly Georgie was gone. That left her in a deep state of grief and despondency. But through this bond of divine love, Georgie came back. He came back to show Linda that there is more to life than she had ever known before.

Georgie existed because he was Soul, and Soul exists because God loves It. That is why there is no such thing as eternal death. The teachings of Eckankar give hope to people who have no hope.

Sometimes people are threatened, "Believe this or that or you're going to suffer eternal damnation." There is no eternal damnation.

There are purgatories where people go for a time between lifetimes where they work out some of the more overt problems they have caused by breaking the Law of Karma. But these aren't eternal. Soul is eternal, and purgatory belongs to the lower worlds, which are perishable.

God is love, and Soul exists because God loves It.

The lower heavens will someday perish, and these include the worlds of the Causal Plane where Linda saw the personalities going down the slide of reincarnation. These things will all perish someday.

But not Soul. Nor divine love. God is love, and Soul exists because God loves It.

PAUL TWITCHELL'S MISSION

Linda knew this after her experience with Georgie. But it was still some time before she found the teachings of ECK.

In about 1967 she was pregnant with her second child. Once a week she'd take out her ironing board and iron the laundry while she watched a TV show she liked.

It was called the Joe Pyne Show. Joe Pyne was a crude, abrasive person who insulted his guests. He would be seated onstage, and a guest would come up from the audience to be interviewed. Then Joe Pyne would insult the guest. This was his shtick, his spiel. The audience was composed of people who loved to see him insult these guests. Often the guests were a little offbeat, from strange professions like fortune-telling. The whole show was offbeat.

Linda had the TV on that night while she did her ironing; she was kind of singing to herself, happy that her baby was going to be born soon, waiting for her show to come on.

The show came on, and in the middle of it a little man in the audience stood up and said he was a spiritual leader of this religion. Joe Pyne said, "Well, come on up here and let's talk."

Paul Twitchell had an incredibly difficult job.

He tried to get information out of this man, who turned out to be Paul Twitchell, the modern-day founder of Eckankar.

Paul Twitchell had an incredibly difficult job. He had to somehow bring the ECK teachings to the world in a short period of time; he had to somehow catch the attention of the public with these ancient teachings of the Light and Sound of God.

Picture a racetrack. Way down the track are all these other teachings, the various religions of one kind or another. They are already way down the track, and back at the starting gate is this little man called Paul Twitchell. He hasn't even started running yet. How's he going to catch up? How is he going to let anybody know about these teachings of Light and Sound, these teachings of divine love? How's he going to do it? I think Paul was scratching his head, too, trying to figure out what to do.

So he thought he would get himself on this show, even though he knew he was really going to take a licking.

AN UNEXPECTED VEHICLE

Paul was invited onstage, and the talk-show host interviewed him. Everything went intolerably bad, as you'd expect on a show like this. Then Paul mentioned that his role as a spiritual leader was to help people leave the cycle of karma and reincarnation. Joe Pyne said, "You mean you're like Jesus Christ."

Paul said, "Well, my function is to help Souls out of this world."

When he heard this, Joe Pyne let Paul have it with both barrels. He was just abusive. And it was at this point that something changed in Linda as she watched the show.

She used to like this interviewer, how he'd get up there and run his guests over the hot coals to see how they'd jump over them and try to escape back to the safety of the audience. But Paul took the abuse very quietly, in a very gentle manner. And as Linda watched, she said, "What right does Joe Pyne have to abuse this gentle, sweet little man like this?" She could see he was a good man. Her sympathies went out to Paul because of who and what he was.

After the show went off the air, Linda totally forgot about Paul Twitchell. Some years later, she finally found the teachings of ECK.

And as she looked back, she wondered how many people who later got into ECK had their first introduction to the teachings of Light and Sound on the Joe Pyne show when they saw Paul Twitchell. How many of them probably didn't remember it later? For all I know, it could've been me, too, except I was overseas then.

THE X-GENERATION

Today there is some talk about the X-generation, our children, the next generation. They don't know where to go, what to do. They're facing the prospects of a worse future than we had. But when I was in my twenties, I didn't have a prayer. I faced service in Vietnam unless I enlisted in the Air Force. And everyone knew that if you went to Vietnam, your chances of coming home in one piece weren't very good.

This was a fever, a war fever, that had swept our government. This fever was sending the young men over there. Some of us who didn't know any better were caught in the squeeze, trying to figure out the best course of action to take to come out of it in one piece.

The X-generation today has it so good, yet the media is creating this false image that the youth are facing a worse future than we faced.

I faced no future at all. A lot of my friends in service were also afraid of going to Vietnam. Of course there were others in the service who couldn't wait to get there.

The X-generation hasn't suffered very much. They are people who have maybe made the jump from one job to another and are bitterly disappointed that they haven't become president of the company. Now they're trying to figure out how to sue the company and get what's rightfully theirs.

Life shall teach you better. If you don't get it now, you'll get it later.

You put an X in front of the generation, in front of all those who feel that way, and then just forget about them. Except that you can't. It's a whole wave of people who don't understand the Law of Cause and Effect; as a group, they don't understand personal responsibility.

But life shall teach them better. That is one of my favorite sayings. If you don't get it now, you'll get it later.

BETWEEN A ROCK AND A HARD PLACE

A young woman lived in a city where she had no close family, no friends, no mate, no job. She had recently lost both her boyfriend and her job. And so she felt she had nothing to live for. She'd become suicidal, trying to figure out how to get up enough courage to leap off the balcony of the seventeenth-floor apartment where she lived. She felt life held nothing for her.

The woman used to spend her days walking in the park, walking in a dismal state of despondency, wondering what did life hold, what did life have to offer.

This, of course, happened long before the X-generation. She didn't have anything. She wasn't surrounded by a loving family and friends. The generation today overlooks all the blessings they have and says, "Why don't I have more? Why don't I have more of what everyone else has? And why do I have to work for it?" It's a spiritual sickness that has hit at least the American society.

This woman truly did have hardships. She was between a rock and a very hard place and didn't know what to do.

BUTTERSCOTCH SUNDAES

The young woman didn't eat very much, but one of her favorite foods was ice cream with butterscotch syrup and walnuts on top. This was her favorite snack, her favorite meal—it was what she lived on.

You know, ice cream is a dairy product, so it's got to be healthy, right? And nuts? Nuts are healthy. So this was what she ate. It was her source of nutrition.

She used to go to a very busy delicatessen near a subway exit. Crowds of people would run in there, pick up their take-out lunches, and run home to their loved ones or back to their job. But this woman didn't race up to the counter. She wasn't like the people who stood three or four deep, raising their arms over their heads, trying to catch the clerk's eye so they could get along with their lives.

She didn't have anyone. So she just waited in the back until there was a lull in business.

This woman had been a bank clerk. She knew that to be successful a clerk needed to make eye contact with only the person just in front of him. She had learned never to look at the whole crowd and get flustered, but to serve that one person and only that person.

Otherwise you were prone to making mistakes. And if you made mistakes, especially when it had to do with money, the bank management would probably ask you to make up the difference. And if you made too many mistakes because of the mob trying to get through the bank line at lunch hour, if you got flustered, the bank might even fire you.

GIFT OF LOVE

One day the woman was standing in line at the deli, having picked out her ice cream, butterscotch syrup, and walnuts. She was feeling very despondent, without love, without hope, as if she would just drag on through this life. She waited and waited, but there was no lull in the mob in front of the counter that day.

So she held up her arms, just held them up with the things she wanted to buy, moving closer to the counter where a clerk could wait on her.

The clerks were middle-aged women, and they had to take a lot of abuse from the customers. The customers were demanding, wanting to be served right now. The clerks would take one customer after another, throw their purchases into a little white bag, run up to the till, ring up the sale, then take the change back to the customer. Then they'd wait on the next customer. All day long this would go on.

The young woman stood there until her arms ached. Finally she caught the eye of one of the clerks. The clerk took her purchases, threw them in the white bag, took her money, ran to the till, came back with the change.

And in this clamor of people all around them, the clerk suddenly looked into the eyes of this young woman.

Then she stopped and looked deeper, looked into the eyes of Soul, looked all the way into the heart of this young woman for a moment.

Wrapped slices of cake were lying on the counter. And without a word, the clerk picked up one of these wrapped slices of cake and put it into the bag for free. It was as if she were reaffirming the look of love that had passed between herself and this young woman who was way down on her luck, perhaps in the deepest state of despondency she'd ever been in. It was as if she was assuring the young woman that yes, this was a look of love.

And before the young woman could even say thanks, the clerk was off and running to serve another customer.

The young woman never saw the clerk again, but an important thing happened to her in that moment. As she went home, there was love in her heart for the first time. Someone had passed the gift of love to her. It didn't cost a thing. There was no money connected with the look of love or the slice of cake that went with it.

It was a gift from the heart.

From this time on, the young woman began to

have hope. She had a feeling of lightness she hadn't felt in a very long time. The next day, she went out and began to look for better, more nutritious food than she'd been eating. And it wasn't long after that she found another job and another love interest. Her life got back on track.

Many years later, the woman found the teachings of ECK. She realized that this one experience in the delicatessen was a turning point in her life because someone had bothered to give her the gift of love through simply looking directly into her eyes.

THE HOPE OF THE GOLDEN HEART

Sometimes the most precious gift you can give another is as simple as passing along a gift of love.

This is the Year of Giving. And sometimes the most precious gift you can give another is as simple as passing along a gift of love. Just looking at Soul standing there, way back in there, behind the physical eyes of the human being who is depressed and down on their luck.

These are the lessons of love and thanks I would like to leave with you.

When I look at the stories of different people as they make their way back home to God, sometimes the tears fall from my eyes too. Because Soul, when It is cut off from the love of God, is in the darkest of times.

And only when the love of God comes to light the golden heart is there a way, is there hope and lightness. There is a chance, then, to make something useful of this life, to go forward with joy and hope. To say, "I know today is rough, but I know there's a tomorrow. And with my own efforts and with the help of the Inner Master, I can make it a better tomorrow."

Because this life is a precious one. You get one

lifetime at a time; make it the best you can.

This woman learned that giving love is the first step to receiving love. To get love you must give. To get love, you must give love wherever and whenever you can, because that is the Law of Love.

I enjoy these meetings with you. But the greater meetings that can occur are the ones where we will meet on the inner planes. Here, I only come once a year. Maybe in future years, I won't be able to come to Australia every year.

But on the inner planes, I am always with you. My love is with you.

To get love, you must give love wherever and whenever you can, because that is the Law of Love.

ECK South Pacific Seminar, Sydney, Australia, Sunday, November 28, 1993

Do all you have agreed to do, and do not encroach on other persons or their property. These two laws are a simple way of living in peace and justice with your neighbor; they also help you recognize when other people are not treating you fairly.

7

RECOGNIZING GOD'S BLESSINGS

*I*n some talks I gave recently, I mentioned how we could recognize God's blessings. Recognizing God's blessings for us also means having to recognize God's blessings for other people. Because where our freedoms begin—and this works both ways—others' end. And where others' begin, ours end.

A SPIRITUAL RULE OF THUMB

How can you come up with a rule of thumb you can use to know when you are giving other people their spiritual freedom and when they are giving you yours? At recent talks I spoke about the two laws, which are an extension of the spiritual law.

The Ten Commandments are very good. But in today's world, are there rules that everyone can agree on?

Richard Maybury has researched and distilled the basic laws and codes that people can use to live in peace and justice with each other. Then he wrote *Whatever Happened to Justice?* I mentioned this book at two recent seminars, and everybody wanted to order the book from its very small publisher. And the

Recognizing God's blessings for us also means having to recognize God's blessings for other people.

119

publisher was swamped.

Two days ago as I was preparing for the talk this morning, I got a package in the mail. It was a T-shirt. On the front is a picture of a woman holding the scales of justice in one hand and a sword in the other. This is the old symbol for justice.

Do all you have agreed to do, and do not encroach on other persons or their property.

On the back are the two laws: Do all you have agreed to do, and do not encroach on other persons or their property.

These are two laws that Richard Maybury came across. They are laws of Spirit; you don't make them up. He discovered them, and he's very humble in his recognition of this. These two laws are a simple way of living in peace and justice with your neighbor; they also help you recognize when other people are not treating you fairly.

I'm not getting into all the details of what each of these two laws means. It's like a legal document: You can have two simple points, but then come the asterisks and the footnotes. And by the time you've finished, you say, "Why, this covers a lot." And these two laws do indeed cover a lot. They're not totally comprehensive, but they are a very good start for those who want to know how to live the spiritual life.

SUNDAY SERVICES

About two weeks ago, I called some relatives, and the phone call went three and a half hours. The phone bill ran to forty dollars. You have to understand: my long-distance phone bill the month before this was thirty cents. I told my wife, "It's going to be months before I make another long-distance call. Months."

The phone call started very nicely. The person mentioned that they had just been to church service.

They're Lutherans. I try to support their religion;

I try to support all good religions and all people who live a religion honestly and well. As we talked, I also told her about our worship services.

We don't have worship services every Sunday necessarily. Some ECK centers in different parts of the country do, but here at the Temple of ECK, we have our worship service once a month. I explained to this relative that the reason we do it this way is that we recognize God's blessing all the time. We have our worship service once a month out of respect for and in recognition of the changing times today.

We recognize God's blessing all the time.

Religions that have been around for centuries were established at a time when the pace of life was much slower and people all lived in the immediate area, either in the town or the community.

For them, church was more than just simply getting spiritual food. It was also a way to share with each other socially.

I grew up in the country, and after the church service all the farmers would gather outside and talk about crops. Which pesticide to use next, how the corn was coming, did it look like the corn was going to be knee high by July fourth. If it was, there was a good chance the corn was going to be a good crop and so on and so forth. They talked about this because the church, besides being a spiritual center, was also a social center.

But today people have less time. As our tax rates keep going up, there's less money for us to spend as we would like.

If there are two people in the household who are of working age, both work to maintain their lifestyle. Today there are also many single-parent households, and it's very tough. People simply do not have the time they did centuries ago for the custom of having

church services once a week. So when we were es-
tablishing our worship services here at the Temple
of ECK a couple years ago, I said once a month is
enough, in deference to the changing needs of today.
We can have other classes each Sunday, but we'll
have a major worship service only once a month.

SOUL IS A LIGHT OF GOD

People certainly shouldn't come here because they
feel guilty if they don't come. That's not the purpose
of God's love and God's blessings.

It shouldn't be that if you're not at the worship
service, other people look at you through social eyes
instead of spiritual eyes and say, "Ah, so-and-so didn't
come today. I wonder where they are." And if you are
the one who didn't show up, you feel guilty. This is
wrong.

*You are Soul.
You are a
light of God.*

With God's love, there should be none of this guilt,
none of these dirty feelings. It's your relationship
with God that counts.

You are Soul. You are a light of God. And whatever your relationship with God is, that is your
relationship with God, and it's your business. Not
anyone else's. We don't try to put a guilt trip on people
and say, "You have to attend the worship service, and
you have to be there so many times."

SMOOTHING FEATHERS

So on the phone with this relative, our conver-
sation had started to go in this direction, and I
mentioned, "We have worship services once a month."

And very stiffly this reply came back, "We think
it's important to give God at least one hour of our time
each week." I thought, *Wow, here we are into numbers.*

It's family, so you don't get into arguments un- necessarily. I didn't try to get very logical and say, "OK, you must be four times more spiritual than we are because you go to church four times a month and we go only once a month." I wanted to say, "But on the other hand, the people of Islam have formal worship, or prayer sessions, five times every day. Does this make them thirty-five times more spiritual than you?" But by then I was losing track, trying to multiply thirty-five times four.

When you carry logic beyond a certain point, it gets to be silly. I thought, *Better let this go.*

So I just said, "You must have a very good min- ister. The people must like him very much because you have a growing congregation."

"Yes, well, that's true," she said.

I smoothed the feathers. You don't want to get into political or religious arguments with your rela- tives. It's often bad enough as it is.

WHO'S MORE SPIRITUAL?

In the New Testament there's the story of the publican and the Pharisee. The Pharisee makes a big show of worship, he lets everybody know he's wor- shiping. The publican, very quietly, goes into the closet to pray.

The publican is very humble; he prays in the closet. But everybody thinks very highly of the Pharisee.

When I heard my relative's stiff, stilted tone on the telephone, I thought, *How do I defend the fact that we have worship service once a month, and somebody else has it once a week?*

So who's more spiritual? You can't tell outwardly. You can't even tell in any other way. How is a human being to judge the spiritual state of another human being? Each human being would judge someone else through the bias that each person naturally carries. A person might think, *I've gone to church every Sunday, and that is the right way to do it.* Well, that's a bias. Maybe it's not the right way to do it.

How is a human being to judge the spiritual state of another human being?

I've known some very fine people who were called atheists. They felt they loved and worshiped God, but they didn't go to church on Sunday. So they were outcasts in the community back home. People are not logical when it comes to feelings. And religion for most people is based on feelings.

It's the same with politics. People become very angry and very heated about these things.

So if you can, practice the two laws when you're in the presence of these people. Just give them love, and don't push the argument. Let them be. Let them have their space, even though they don't have the spiritual awareness to give you your space.

People don't realize that God has provided all these different religions for a specific purpose: to fit all the different levels of consciousness that exist on earth.

RELIGIOUS PURPOSE

I find, whenever possible, it's better to build others up. Because all religions are from God. This is one of the simple truths that very few people recognize or understand.

All religions are from God, but we like to say, "My religion is directly from God." And that means that everybody else's is some splinter or shade less than truth. People don't realize that God has provided all these different religions for a specific purpose: to fit all the different levels of consciousness that exist on earth. Somebody who is a good, practicing Lutheran may have an entirely different set of ethics from someone who practices Islam.

People who are in the top 5 percent of any religious group—if you're going to grade them by spirituality or closeness to God—have very much in common. They are generally people who are filled with love. They are people who know the two laws that I told you about.

They understand that just obeying laws, following the letter of the law, is not living in the heart of God.

The point of any religion should be this: how to open your heart to love. Because God is love. And if you can achieve that through the religion you're in now, the religion is right for you. But if your heart is not opening to love, then the religion is not right for you. Or let's say it another way: you're not right for that religion.

The point of any religion should be this: how to open your heart to love.

TEMPLE OF GOD WITHIN YOU

When I was talking to this relative and she said, "We go to church once a week," I said, "Yes, but we feel we are in the presence of God every minute."

This caught her off guard. After a moment, she said, "Well, of course, we do too."

And this is the whole point. No outer building is the temple of God. No outer temple can be more sacred than the temple of God within you. If the temple of God is very sacred to you, you can come into any building and that building will be as sacred as the temple is within your heart. Because this temple is the one that reflects your relationship with God.

Are you filled with love? Then your temple is good and strong. Are you filled with nit-picking, criticisms, and all the other children of anger? Then you still have something to learn, either in the present religion you're in or another one. My feeling is that if you are having problems with anger and all these other things, please work them out in your own religion before you come to ECK.

We have enough problems trying to learn and remember how to live and be in the presence of God every minute.

SOUL'S NATURAL HOME

Earth makes sure it's not easy. In fact, people often wonder, *What's the purpose for Satan or the devil or whatever you want to call this negative power?* It's to make you more spiritual.

Every Soul is of God. You cannot separate yourself from God eternally.

This is one of the simpler truths that a lot of religions overlook. Its purpose is not to try to tear you from God, because in the long run, that's impossible. Every Soul is of God. You cannot separate yourself from God eternally. You can, short term. You may end up in a temporary hell or purgatory—either in this world or the next. But long term, every Soul is of God. In the high worlds where there is not this dual element of good and evil, everything is just simply God's love. And that is the natural home for Soul.

Of course there are some very negative people here who do some very bad things. And they're going to pay for them, because that is the Law of Cause and Effect, or the Law of Karma. They'll pay in their own way and in the true coin. Why? Because that's God's law. And surprisingly, it's God's Law of Love.

WHY ARE WE HERE?

Why are people here? Why are we here? To learn to open our hearts completely to love. Why? Because once we do that, we can become a clear Co-worker with God. To do what? Sometimes just to listen to other people who are weighed down by the burdens of the day, broken relationships, or the death of a loved one.

Sometimes being a Co-worker with God means just to listen to someone else. When they come to you because they need to talk, you have to have the awareness to just simply listen to them.

This is one of the golden gifts of the people who are Co-workers with God: the ability to listen to others. When people are in trouble, they don't need to hear how smart you are. They don't need all kinds of words of wisdom.

The greatest wisdom and the greatest love you can show someone else is simply to listen when they're in very bad trouble.

RECOGNIZING GOD'S BLESSINGS

Recognizing God's blessings may come in many different ways. Sometimes it's a simple thing.

Over the holidays, my wife and I went out to eat. Trying to find a place to eat is quite a trick because they're all crowded and you have to call ahead for reservations. But we found a place that wasn't very crowded.

As I get older, I have to watch my diet more than I did before. When I was younger, I could eat anything and considered it all health food. French-fried potatoes are potatoes, healthy because they are potatoes from God's sweet earth. And ice cream and malts and the like are from God's gift of milk. And sugar—that's a natural product. Pastry is made from the grains of the earth.

Doctors say it isn't good for you to eat that sort of thing. I found as I get older, my body tells me that I have to cut down on fat. I simply don't feel good if I eat too much of it. I have this feeling of unwellness.

This is one of the golden gifts of the people who are Co-workers with God: the ability to listen to others.

So over the holidays I'd been watching my fat intake very carefully, because I feel better when I do. And we came up to the buffet. I said, "Well, a little gravy couldn't hurt me." But gravy has a lot of fat in it. A lot of fat.

WHAT'S THE TIE-IN?

I carried my plate back to the table. My wife was still at the buffet. I set it down, very carefully. That day I had my suit on and my favorite—and practically only—tie. I had just gotten it cleaned. I'm very picky about clean clothes. My wife and I are the kind of people who, when we see lint on each other, we take it off. Half the people in the world are that way. The other half aren't. So half of you will understand. The other half of you won't.

So, as I sat down, my tie very neatly and gracefully dragged itself right through the gravy. Notice how I worded that so I have no responsibility for what happened.

I'm sitting there trying to wipe my tie clean on my napkin, which is a stiff piece of cloth that doesn't absorb anything. I'm sitting there with this sad look on my face, and my wife came back. She likes to play on words. She said, "What's the tie-in?"

I said, "I guess the tie's in with gravy, isn't it?"

Divine Spirit, or the ECK, was trying to tell me that I have my own rules for how much fat I can take and that I was taking too much this time.

I realized too late that Divine Spirit, or the ECK, was trying to tell me that I have my own rules for how much fat I can take and that I was taking too much this time. So I scraped the gravy off to the side, sort of. You know how we fudge on things. You say, "Well, I'm scraping most of it off. I'm listening. I'm listening, Spirit."

And after I finished, I went up to the table and I got some cake. I thought it looked kind of light—

more or less. Like angel food cake. *Light color,* I thought, *maybe it's kind of light.* It was really good, too, so I went back and had another piece.

OUR PERSONAL CODES

But I had my warnings. This was one of the blessings of the Divine Spirit. It was telling me something through the waking dream. By dragging my tie through the gravy and my wife coming up just then, the image from the divine ECK flashed through my mind. It said, "What's the tie-in?" "Oh, yeah," I said, "with fat. I'm eating too much fat." But then I ate everything anyway.

And then for a couple of days I didn't feel well at all. I felt like I had violated my own dietary code. I ate something I shouldn't have. I suffered and paid for it.

This is another of the ways that Divine Spirit will tell us we're doing something that's against our own code. It wasn't up to my wife or the doctor to tell me. I try to listen to Divine Spirit so that I don't end up in really bad circumstances.

Life will tell you what's right for you, and it will also tell you what's wrong for you.

Life will tell you what's right for you, and it will also tell you what's wrong for you. We call this the waking dream or the Golden-tongued Wisdom.

It can be something as simple as a tie dragging through the gravy. This is going to catch your attention. You say, "Oh, what a mess! Is this tie ruined?"

Sometimes the blessings of God are so down-to-earth that we overlook them. We think God is looking out for our spiritual good, this intangible thing that we can't quite put our finger on. We figure it must mean moral codes. Mark Twain once said that people prize sex so much, it's odd they would leave it out of their heaven. On earth, the moral code becomes "the

Sometimes people can actually see the Light in contemplation, or they can hear the Sound of God in some way.

code." But there are other codes. There are ethical codes. There are dietary codes. There are attitude codes: How do we look at life? There are such things as taking the problems of the day in stride or letting them twist us into a nervous wreck. These are codes too.

These all come under the hand, or direction, of the Holy Spirit. I speak of the Holy Spirit here as the Voice of God. In Eckankar, we are the Religion of the Light and Sound of God. This Voice of God speaks most directly and most clearly to Soul through the Light and Sound.

Sometimes people can actually see the Light in contemplation, or they can hear the Sound of God in some way. Sometimes it's the sound of a bird, a musical instrument, a train.

SALAD BAR STORY

One of the ECKists wrote to me recently, and he said he had gone to a restaurant where you get a free salad with the entrée. So when the waiter came, he ordered the entrée and the waiter said, "You can help yourself to the salad bar."

While the ECKist was helping himself to the salad, a boy of ten came up to him and very timidly asked, "Can I have some of that too?"

"You can ask the waiter," said the ECKist.

But the ten-year-old didn't feel comfortable with that. He was afraid to ask the waiter. So the ECKist called the waiter over and said, "Can this young gentleman also have the salad bar?"

"Sure," the waiter said. "It comes with his entrée."

Later the waiter told the ECKist, "This boy's mother often brings him over here, just drops him off in the restaurant by himself while she goes shopping in the mall." So this little boy was often stranded there, and he didn't really know who to ask. He thought he could only have the entrée his mother paid for, only what was on his plate.

But over the weeks he had been watching other people. They would get their plates and go to the salad bar. And the little boy began to think, *Maybe I could do that too.*

So on this particular day he saw the ECKist, who seemed a friendly person of good heart. And the little boy had the courage to go up to him. The ECKist said to the boy, "You can have everything you can see." This made the little boy really happy. Suddenly his time in the restaurant took on a different light.

It was one of God's blessings. He wasn't just stuck with what was on his plate.

"I FEEL SO RICH"

After the boy had finished eating, he came up to the ECKist and said, "I feel so rich." He said this several times.

He was so happy that this ECKist had found out what he needed to know because until then, the boy didn't realize that he could have anything he saw in the salad bar. He could partake of all God's blessings within the restaurant.

Life is like that too. There is so much that God has to give you and me. But all these different rules and codes that we live by sometimes restrict us in the wrong way without letting us know that there is a higher law. It is the Law of Divine Love.

These codes can keep us from seeing that all God's blessings are for us, as long as we remember these two laws that I mentioned before, as long as we do not enjoy God's blessings at the expense of

God's blessings are always with you. You just need the eyes to see and the ears to hear.

someone else.

God's blessings are always with you. You just need the eyes to see and the ears to hear. We're speaking of the Light and Sound of God—the visual and the auditory—to see and hear God's blessings. Because if you can open your heart with love, you can tune in to God's will.

If you can open your heart with love, you can tune in to God's will.

And as you do, you will find life begins to take on meaning, beyond anything you've ever heard or felt before. In other words, you're going to tune in to truth, divine truth. You will become a sincere truth seeker of the highest order.

So I'd like to leave you with the blessings of the Vairagi ECK Masters. May the blessings be.

Temple of ECK Worship Service, Chanhassen, Minnesota, February 6, 1994

The man who'd always wanted a beagle but could never find one in the pet stores was the only one who could get near the frightened dog.

8
BLESS THIS DAY

elcome to the ECK Springtime Seminar here in the beautiful city of San Diego. It's a lot of fun looking out the window at the ships going back and forth. There's a good feeling or maybe a memory of a long time ago, of good times and bad times sailing on the sea of life.

Often we overlook the blessings of the day.

Sometimes life carries us along so fast that we don't have time to think about the moment. Often we overlook the blessings of the day.

We're always thinking, *What do I have to do today? After work I've got to shop. And after I finish shopping, then I have to get dinner.* Things go so fast that sometimes we're in a constant whirl, a whirl of unconscious living. And if someone asks us, "What did you like about today?" we look back at them and say, "What do you mean? Today was like any other."

PLANTING TREES

A woman recently lost her job because the company folded. There's been a lot of that going on despite the economic recovery. You say, "Recovery? Somebody's recovering?" I'm not sure where or what.

After this woman lost her job, she ended up at home planting some trees with her neighbor's help.

Her eighty-three-year-old neighbor is an energetic man. He likes to work but won't accept any money. He's always offering to help people do this or that project. While they were putting in the trees, they also had to add a water line. So this old gentleman had offered to help with that too.

He was digging to find the existing water line, and he missed. He dug for quite a distance before he found out he wasn't going to cross the water line but was running parallel to it.

Later he was digging holes for the trees, and the woman was digging too. She's a middle-aged woman. And she was trying to keep up with this elderly man. At the end of the day when her husband came home, the woman said, "He works so hard. I just couldn't keep up with this eighty-three-year-old man."

But when her husband went over and talked to him later, the neighbor said, "You know, I had just the hardest time keeping up with her."

BLESS THIS DAY

During the day, the old gentleman had come to her and said, "Why don't you go home and take a rest?" because he needed to. But she didn't know that, so she said, "No, when you offered to help, I didn't plan to have you do all the work. No, I'm going to stay."

She kept digging, trying to keep up with him. And he tried to keep up with her. And they both practically destroyed each other.

Finally the stories came together, and they got a little laugh out of it. But it's one of those times when you look back and say, "Bless this day." Why? Because these people were giving to each other, just giving to each other, sharing work.

There were elements in this game plan neither knew about: such as doing it to please each other, to work hard and not be the slacker. They were both pushing themselves a little bit too far. But everything worked out, and so at the end—if they had wanted to, if they had thought to, if they hadn't been too tired—they could have said, "Bless this day."

"Bless this day."

INDIVIDUAL RIGHTS

Coming over on the plane, I found the flight attendants to be courteous, very efficient, good people. But sometimes when people have to work so fast and hard to serve others, they can forget that people are people and not things.

We were seated on the plane next to a woman who was in her seventies. She had a lot more energy than I have. She was going to go to Disneyland. She was taking one of these flights where you hop, skip, and jump across the country. Her son was some important official at Disneyland.

Then the beverage cart started coming down the aisle, and my wife ordered something for me and also for herself. The flight attendant asked the elderly woman by the window what she wanted. And she said, "Coffee; cream and sugar, please."

The flight attendant called back to the other person bringing the coffee, "Window wants coffee, cream, and sugar."

I get very sensitive about the fact that I am a human being, that I am an individual, a person. And whether other people think it or not, I know I count for something. If to no one else, I count to myself—

and that counts for a lot. Because it's good to wake up in the morning and say, "What a beautiful morning. It's good to be alive." Anyone who can say that, counts. And if the only person who can say it is ourselves, then we'll say it. And then we count.

So I turned to the little woman at the window, and I said, "She called you a window."

This woman was so sweet. Never offended. When she had to go to the toilet, she apologized profusely, because my wife and I had notes and stuff spread out all over our tray tables and our laps. We said, "No, no. It's all right. We're used to this. We can clean this up, and we can be out of here in a second. Just get your stuff together and be ready to jump out." She was so polite.

So I said to her, "You're not a window. You're a person." I was doing this in a stage whisper, the kind that carries—far.

And I have to give the flight attendant credit; she really did have a good sense of humor. She called back to the one at the first cart, "The lady by the window. Coffee, cream, and sugar, please." And then the flight attendant smiled very brightly to us and moved down the aisle to serve some of the other passengers.

Sometimes when things get so fast, we forget that it's a plane filled with people, a plane filled with individuals. And if there weren't any individuals, there wouldn't be any need for the plane. And if there weren't individuals, there wouldn't be any need for towns. There wouldn't be any use for nations.

We are here on this earth with the opportunity to go home to God.

Individuals are very important. They're all important because individually, you and I are Soul, we're lights of God. We are here on this earth with the opportunity to go home to God.

GROCERY LINES

I've noticed that whenever I go into a grocery store, get my things, and am just about ready to check out, somebody announces, "All checkers to the front, please." And you know what that means. It means there are a lot of people up there. Sure enough, when I walk up there, the lines are all very long. I know I'm in for a long wait.

I've learned to plan really carefully before I go in a store. It's as if this store has a consciousness which is just as individual as the people in it. As I run into the store and grab things from the shelves, I know I've got about seven minutes. After about seven minutes, the store sends a message to all the people in there. "OK, time to get up to the checkout stands and form lines. He's coming."

I try not to take these things personally. But I do notice.

It's good to have the strength and the health to be able to go out and shop for food, just to have the strength to walk there.

CROSSING THE STREET

A couple of years ago I had an auto accident, and I was quite sick afterward. My wife was doing all the driving. I didn't walk very much, but when I did, I found it was a real effort, which was unusual because I used to enjoy walking. I used to walk and walk and walk. I thought, *I'll probably keep right on walking when I'm ninety or a hundred; the last thing to go will be my legs.*

Well, one day my wife was in the dentist's chair, and I didn't want to sit in the waiting room; I needed the sunshine. Our dentist is a good man. We like to visit with him. And she was visiting, so I told her I was just going to go for a walk.

On my walk I had to cross a busy street with a traffic light. When you're a driver, you don't often end up crossing the busy streets on foot. Before the accident, I'd always drive places and seldom did I have to walk across a street. If I was going to get across the street, I'd get in my car and drive across the street. What's a car for, after all?

But now, walking in a weakened condition, I found the street wasn't just an ordinary two-lane street. It looked like it was eight lanes across. And the cars all seemed to be going about fifty or sixty.

I felt like a turtle trying to cross the street. Worse, as I got halfway across, I got a little worried. I asked myself, *Am I going to make it across the street?*

I realized what it is like for people who are seventy, eighty, or ninety, or who are ill. What a tremendous challenge it can be for them to do the simplest things that most of us take for granted every day. It gave me a sense of gratitude — if I had thought to say it then. If I knew I was going to be preparing a talk with the title "Bless This Day," I would have probably said, "Bless this day," once I got on the other curb. I barely made it. I couldn't believe it. There's a skill to being a pedestrian — something I had forgotten.

THE NEW DOG

An assistant attorney in the state attorney's office told me a story. When he was a young boy, he had a beagle. He liked beagles. His daughter had dragged him into the pet store a couple of times to look at the puppies. As fathers will, he went.

But he didn't care much about going into the pet stores because they didn't have any beagles. They had every other kind of dog but they never had any beagles.

But we are individuals. And sometimes, without our knowing it, life has a plan for us—a plan for individuals to come together. We may call them coincidences. We think we just chose a certain mate or a certain pet. But often we don't realize that many of these so-called choices have already been made long before. We get an unconscious glimpse of what's to come, and as Soul we begin to make preparations beforehand.

We get an unconscious glimpse of what's to come, and as Soul we begin to make preparations beforehand.

But our preparations look totally foolish to the mind because they don't make any sense. We don't have all the other parts that go with the plan.

One day the man had this strong urge to go to a grocery store, and when he got there, he said, "Hey, I'll pick up a bag of dog food." That's pretty unusual for someone who doesn't have a dog. As he lugged this dog food out to the car, he was wondering, *What am I going to do with this dog food? I don't have a dog.*

FINDING EACH OTHER

About two weeks later, as he was going into the courthouse one morning, the man saw a beagle running around outside the building. It looked lost and afraid, very confused. So the man went inside and called the animal control people.

As they were waiting for the animal control people to get there, the man and some of his friends tried to catch the dog. It was winter, but the dog didn't want to be caught. In fact, they later found out that the animal control people had been trying for days to catch this dog.

As the men were chasing the dog, it ran across a pond that wasn't frozen solid. The dog got to the middle of the pond and fell in.

The beagle managed to pull himself out of the freezing water. He reached the ice on the other side of the hole, and he pulled and pulled until he got himself out. The dog staggered across the ice to the shore, but at that point he couldn't go a step farther. He fell underneath a bush and collapsed.

And the man who'd always wanted a beagle but could never find one in the pet stores was the only one who could get near the frightened dog.

But the animal control people wanted the dog; they'd been chasing it for days.

"They're not going to get this dog," the man said. He had fought so hard for the dog. He didn't know exactly how he was going to keep him out of the pound, but he was going to try.

The man just happened to see a friend of his, not realizing that this woman used to be president of the local Humane Society. "I've got to find a way to keep this dog," he told her. And she said, "I'll see what I can do." A little while later he got a call from the animal control people; they said he could keep the dog.

The two individuals, man and dog, were looking for each other. They had to get together.

COINCIDENCES

This worked out through a series of coincidences. The man thought that he just happened to be at the courthouse where this dog was running around. But what he didn't know was this: the two individuals, man and dog, were looking for each other. They had to get together. So the former president of the Humane Society removed all the obstacles, and the man could take the dog home.

There came one final thing. He had to name the dog. Some people suggested calling him Lucky because he had come out of the ice and he was fine. But the man thought about it and remembered that somebody had been telling him the story of *Huckleberry Finn,* how the characters in that story had been eluding the law.

"That's just the way it was with this dog," the man said, so he decided to call him Huckleberry. And then later he realized that the first two letters of Huckleberry, of course, are H-U—HU, this name for God.

And now there's a special relationship between the man and the dog. Two individuals came together through a series of coincidences.

Someone in his right mind, like a scientist, would look at this and say, "Yeah, they're just coincidences." But sometimes there is a plan to life that allows things to happen that are supposed to happen.

THE REAL PURPOSE OF LIFE

When we go through a day of hardship or trouble, we say, "Why do these things happen to me? What a terrible day." But it really isn't terrible.

The couple who told me the story of planting the trees mentioned something else to me. If they'd learned one thing in ECK, the husband said, it was that everything happens for a purpose. Even though his wife had lost her job, they still knew this was true. If you know about ECK and the teachings of the Holy Spirit, you know that everything happens for a purpose: to lift Soul higher and give It more experience. So that one day It can become a Co-worker with God.

Everything happens for a purpose: to lift Soul higher and give It more experience.

This is the purpose of Soul. This is why you're here. It's not to endure this life until you die and then go to heaven where everything will be wonderful. That's not what life is about.

The world is filled with individuals — Souls. They're at all different stages or levels of consciousness, each doing what they think is the most important thing for them to do at that very moment. Sometimes people act selfishly. They think they're acting only for their own interest to gain something for themselves. But many times they're inadvertently doing something to benefit other people.

Because this earth—and indeed the worlds beyond earth—is filled with lights of God. Individuals. Most of them don't realize that they, too, are having the experiences in everyday life that will give them what they need—good and bad—to make them fit, someday, to be a Co-worker with God.

WHAT'S A CO-WORKER?

And you say, "Co-worker? Doing what? Being a slave of God or something like this?"

People think being a Co-worker with God could be really dull, especially doing it forever. My point of view is that just lying around in heaven doing nothing for eternity would be worse. But being a Co-worker with God means continuing to develop—not just your creative powers, but your capacity to love. And this goes on and on and on. It's a little hard to explain. Co-workers with God, the ECK Masters, don't see themselves as functionaries in an impersonal way. They are acting as instruments of divine love.

This love of the Holy Spirit, this love of God, pours through them, and they must give it out to others in service. They must give it out because love is life, and life is love.

These ECK Masters are high in consciousness so this love comes pouring through and there is no way they can block it. They must give and give and give. They become a self-fulfilling law of love wherever they go.

Being a Co-worker with God means continuing to develop—not just your creative powers, but your capacity to love.

Sometimes it's just listening to other people tell about their heartaches, their smashed dreams. But other times, it's helping people achieve their goals as they are unconsciously striving to become Co-workers with God. The ECK Masters work in complete consciousness—in full consciousness—of their relationship with God.

Most people do not have this consciousness of their relationship with God. They have beliefs, but beliefs and awareness are not the same thing.

People who belong to other religions believe in the creeds of their religions. The creeds may be right or wrong to varying degrees. But the ECK Masters know what their relationship with God is. They are not God. You do not become one with God, even though you are Soul, a light of God. You become one with the Holy Spirit.

You do not become one with God, even though you are Soul, a light of God. You become one with the Holy Spirit.

READY TO UNDERSTAND

This morning I was talking to a group of people, trying to get some ideas across. Most of the people understood, but a few didn't. I worked at this from several different angles using stories and metaphors, but I'd always hit this blank wall of unconsciousness. So I'd try one more time from another place. And I just couldn't get through—just to a few of the people—because they did not understand, although they believed they understood.

But there's a difference between believing and knowing. They believed they understood. I knew they didn't.

I took extra time trying to use the words that we have, to deal with the limitations of language. I wish I had more beautiful words. I wish I had more ex- pressive words to say what the truth of God is. But let's say I did have them: then there's still the problem of people.

Some people can understand, and others can't because they're not ready. They will be ready in just a couple of weeks, a couple of days, or maybe even a couple of lifetimes.

But whatever the case, I make an effort. Sometimes I try so hard that if I were a person in sales, somebody would accuse me of overselling. I'd keep on talking after the sale is closed. But I wasn't trying to sell anyone on my idea. I was trying to point out the truth of a matter.

EXPERIENCES OF LIFE TEACH TRUTH

The experiences of life teach truth.

When you're working with the illusions that people carry within themselves, it's very difficult—if not impossible—to get through. The only thing that can carry this truth into the hearts of people is the experiences of life. That is why I don't put too much importance on the words I speak. They can be a real shortcut for those of you who care. But for others who have come to a certain level and can't go beyond it, life itself will teach you better. I like to say that, because I've found it is true.

The experiences of life teach truth. Life is not a thing to endure. We don't just put in our time until the last day of our life on earth.

People in Christianity feel the last day comes with final judgment. People have mixed feelings about that final judgment. They don't know if they'd prefer the last day to come to spare them from their dying day, or to have their dying day and just forgo judgment day. They're not sure. It's one of those uncomfortable dilemmas their religion puts them in.

SOUL NEVER DIES

Basically, the instinct of Soul is to live. We want to live. We want to exist. And this is the message of the ECK teachings: that when this body dies, life goes on.

You go on. You are Soul. You are eternal. You exist because God loves you. And you simply wear a body while you're here on earth. When this body has run its course, it's dropped in death. But only the physical body dies. Soul—which means you—continues to live.

And you live on the higher planes or in one of the heavens of God, often with very much the same appearance that you have here except it's a higher and finer body.

I could say that the heavens are all pure joy and happiness. Some of them are, but not all of them are. The heavens just above the Earth Plane have their mixture of good and bad in varying degrees. Earth is at the base of this series of planes of existence. Here there are more rainy days than sunny days, but the higher you go, there are more sunny days and fewer rainy days.

Then at the Soul Plane, which is just above the Mental Plane, you reach the first of the true spiritual worlds. This is where Soul exists in the Light and Sound of God directly.

WHAT ARE THE LIGHT AND SOUND OF GOD?

What are the Light and Sound of God? They are the two aspects that Christianity has called the Holy Spirit. This is the Voice of God.

The Voice of God comes down through creation as Light and Sound. We take these two aspects of life

The Voice of God comes down through creation as Light and Sound.

for granted here. We see the lights around us. We see the sun. We see the moon. We see stage lights and auditorium lights. We take them for granted.

And I guess it's easy to take secondary manifestations of the Light of God for granted. We take the man-made creations, like the lightbulb, for granted because we have them. We're used to them. We can buy them for a dollar or two in the store when we're shopping for groceries.

And if you can buy something in a grocery store, it can't be all that spiritual, can it?

In the late 1800s there were speakers who used to go around the country giving lectures on one thing or another. Sometimes they were humorous speakers such as Mark Twain or Robert Ingersoll, the great agnostic. They drew many thousands of people, and they didn't have the benefit of a microphone as I do. They learned to project their voices.

They were working with sound. According to their state of consciousness, their words had the power to change the consciousness of thousands of people.

When people went to a lecture by Mark Twain, they came away laughing, but they also came away a lot wiser because that man had a rare insight into human nature and the follies of the human state of consciousness. He poked fun at politicians and people. He did this because he loved people so much.

Most of these speakers love people or they wouldn't bother to do it.

KARMIC RETURN

Some, however, misuse this power of speech by trying to control others. Sometimes the human voice is used to control the destiny of nations and to enslave others. This is a misuse of the Sound. Sometimes people use their voices—which are aspects, again, of the Voice of God—by talking ill of others when there is no need to.

This also is the experience of Soul. The seeds we plant come back to us. These things come back.

But most people don't believe that. They don't believe in the principle of karma—the principle of cause and effect—that the things we do come back to us. And when they come back, they educate us, they educate Soul. But often, Soul does not make the connection between cause and effect because the events are too far apart. The cause—where a person broke the spiritual law—and the effect—where the person had to pay the price for breaking the spiritual law—can be days, weeks, months, years, or lifetimes apart.

But gradually, as time goes on and the person comes to a higher state of consciousness, he or she begins to get the dream teachings of ECK. Suddenly you start dreaming about things.

BEATING THE SYSTEM

A woman had a dream about ethics. Up until now, she had been one of those who liked to be a part of ECK because the ECK teachings were so liberal. She was always trying to beat the system—at work, anywhere. She was always trying to get an edge. It wasn't always honest, but she was always trying to beat the system.

One night she had a dream, and she was in a cafeteria. So she went down the line and saw a section of cheeses and vegetables. All the items here were only five cents per ounce. The next section down the line was the meat section. These items were thirty-five cents an ounce, much more expensive.

The seeds we plant come back to us.

As time goes on and the person comes to a higher state of consciousness, he or she begins to get the dream teachings of ECK.

She didn't want to pay for the expensive meat, so she helped herself to some vegetables and some cheeses. As she picked up a piece of cheese, she saw that one of the meats had slipped into the cheese bin.

In her dream, she said, "Hmm, this slice of beef is in the cheese bin. Therefore, it should cost only five cents."

So she put this meat on her plate, packed cheese all around it, put vegetables all on top of that, and hid it very nicely. Then she pushed her tray up to the cashier's register.

Dreams have this way of jumping ahead, creating a blank spot where you don't remember what happened between the register and the table. Next scene, she's seated at the table with the plate in front of her, but the meat's not there.

No matter how small a thing you try to hide, it is known.

Here comes the cashier, with a big smile on her face, bringing napkins. In one napkin is this slice of beef. The cashier smiles, puts it in front of the woman, and the customer knows that, really, she has paid for it.

But the smile said, "No matter how small a thing you try to hide, it is known."

LETTER OF THE LAW

When this ECK initiate woke up, she was horrified. She couldn't believe she had tried to sneak this slice of beef in for one-seventh of the price using the lame excuse "Well, it fell in the cheese bin, so I was just taking things from the cheese bin."

Beating the system is trying to beat the laws of life. It's lying to yourself, and she realized this.

People do this so often. They take the letter of the law, and they break the law; but they use the letter of the law to excuse themselves in their own mind. They say, "I have a right to this because," and add whatever reason it is.

There are many slices of beef in life that are in the wrong tray. And we're always trying to figure out how to justify taking what we haven't earned. And when other people challenge us, the first reaction we have is usually anger. "What right do they have, depriving me?" we say. Me. The big ego.

Maybe the meat in the wrong bin was a test, but these people never see it that way. They try to cheat the law, and later, the spiritual law comes and demands payment. And it usually demands payment when you're least willing and able to pay back.

SPIRITUAL FREEDOM

This is why so many people in our society today seem to be beset by bad luck. We're trying to pass all kinds of laws to protect people from the consequences of their own actions at some time in the past. It's not to say that we can't help those who can't help themselves. But there's a difference between wanting to help those who truly cannot help themselves and helping those who will not help themselves.

In the spiritual worlds, there are no slaves.

When we demand, as a right, something we have not earned, it obligates another person to provide it. And that person becomes our slave.

We're talking about spiritual freedom. In the spiritual worlds, there are no slaves. You do not get ahead by crushing someone else underneath your foot. In the true spiritual worlds, it's a level playing field, and it's always a win-win situation.

Sometimes there is a basis of illusion behind the laws that govern a society, because society's leaders do not understand the spiritual laws of cause and effect.

HOW TO PRAY TO GOD

An ECK initiate was promoted into a job for which she was not qualified. She didn't have the skills because she hadn't gone through the long period of training for this very technical field.

This should have been a situation where she said, "Bless this day. I have a job another day." But every Sunday night before work on Monday, she always asked the Inner Master, "Please help me remember," because her job involved knowing so many details.

We think in our own ignorant state of human consciousness that we know better than the higher law.

She worked in a government office, and there were so many regulations and things that seemed to make no sense to her at all. She didn't realize until later that by directing her attention this way, it was like a directed prayer. It's saying, "God, I have a lot of fears about my job. So I know how we can get rid of these fears, God. Help me to remember. God, if you could do that, then I'll be OK, and then I can bless another day."

This is what people do, because we think in our own ignorant state of human consciousness that we know better than the higher law.

A nation is made up of individuals, individuals who have trouble governing their own lives. And some of these individuals who have trouble governing their own lives then get elected to office and are then able to govern the lives of everybody. But that's earth. It's been that way since human beings organized themselves into societies. There's always been a pecking order. And this pecking order will exist as long as human beings are together in any small group.

There will be inequities. There will be the law of "might makes right." The power to coerce, to force others less strong to do the will of the strong, because it's earth. It's the testing ground of Soul, the place where Soul learns to become a Co-worker with God. It's where we learn patience and tolerance after we have been impatient and intolerant with others.

It comes back. A person is strong while young, he becomes abusive and power hungry, he controls others. And then this person gets old and loses the power, and younger people come in and have control over this individual.

And never do any of the actors in the play realize that they are playing out the spiritual laws of life, of cause and effect.

This woman had this directed prayer, "Please help me remember." But after a series of dreams and inner experiences, she came to a higher state of consciousness. One day as she was doing her spiritual exercises while driving to work in her car, she just said it differently.

She said, "Bless this day and those I serve."

Bless this day and those I serve.

She wasn't directing God anymore. She wasn't telling God how to make her better at her job by helping her remember. She was asking the higher law, the higher power, to help her become a Co-worker with God.

"Bless this day and those I serve," not "those I badger," not "those I bully at the counter." None of those things. But "those I serve."

From then on, the woman found that she had a whole different outlook on her job. She enjoyed it. She began to enjoy going to work. And even more, she found that this maze of government regulations that she had to carry out made sense. She could see them from a higher level. She saw how they tied together.

HOW DOES PRAYER WORK?

The Spindrift Organization of Pennsylvania has done a lot of experiments in the lab trying to prove that prayer works. They set up experiments with plants, and they tried directed prayer. They'd always have a control group. Then they would see if there were any differences in growth of different things.

They did these experiments for a while, and then somebody had an idea. They said, "We've proved now that prayer changes things." In other words, saying to the little plant, "Grow!" "But now let's see if there's a difference between directed prayer and other types." They wanted to look at another kind of prayer, which is nondirected prayer.

Nondirected prayer is more along the lines of "Thy will be done."

Nondirected prayer is more along the lines of "Thy will be done."

So they took a plate with mold on it. And they put it through a quick rinse of alcohol to give the mold a shock, to almost kill it. And then they drew a line right down the center.

Side A was the control side. They wouldn't pray for that side. On side B they asked people to pray for the mold, but not on the order of "Grow, you little green molds, grow!" They didn't do it like that. They just said, "Thy will be done," regarding the B side.

By doing this truly, people are giving goodwill to life. They're passing along the love of God to other people and things.

They found that nondirected prayer worked even better than directed prayer. Then they did other experiments and got the same results: the nondirected prayer was better than telling God what to do. They also found that some kind of attention was better than nothing at all.

MAY THE BLESSINGS BE

In ECK, we have our own kind of nondirected prayer, and this is the blessing of the Vairagi ECK Masters, essentially the same as "Thy will be done." We say, "May the blessings be."

We don't say, "God bless this person," or "God, heal this." It gets very difficult if you have an illness to say, "God, I need more red blood cells. Produce more red blood cells." It may be exactly the wrong thing. You might need more white blood cells.

Directed prayer doesn't work as well because it depends upon the human consciousness and all its ignorance. But nondirected prayer depends upon the divine power, the higher power. It depends upon the power of God. So whether you say "Thy will, not mine, be done," or as we in ECK say, "May the blessings be," this is the proper spiritual way to direct your own life.

You can use it in your own spiritual exercises with your initiate's word that you sing to yourself during contemplation. You can sing your word, but before you start, you can say, "May the blessings be" or "Thy will be done."

If you have a health problem, or if you're having a problem finding work or keeping the job you have, or if you're having a problem with your loved one or someone not so loved—instead of saying, "God, help me be stronger," maybe just try "Thy will be done."

God's love is unconditional love. Soul exists because God loves It.

It's unconditional love that makes such a prayer. And this is important.

What many people don't realize is that God's love, too, is unconditional love. Soul exists because God loves It. That means you exist because God loves you.

Not because you've done anything right. Not because you're here and God owes it to you, and if

God doesn't owe it, we'll pass some laws to make God love us. You know, we're all-powerful with our human laws. We try to become God in using them, and all we do is make each other miserable.

So as I conclude this talk, it's been a good day. I would like to say, "Bless this day." And as we bless this day, we realize it was another opportunity to grow: to see, to know, to be.

These are aspects of Soul: to see, to know, to be. No matter what your age — whether you're a child, whether you're very old and have seen all the seasons of life many, many times — as long as you have the love of God in your heart, you will always have this instinctive urge to see another day, and to say good night to this day as "Bless this day."

ECK Springtime Seminar, San Diego, California,
Friday, April 1, 1994

This word *HU* is the ancient name for God, a love song to God. When Soul has heard this sound, Soul yearns to go home.

9
HU—THE MOST BEAUTIFUL PRAYER
PART 1

*T*he title of the talk this evening is "HU—The Most Beautiful Prayer."

In ECK we enjoy life. We try to live as well as we can, even while we are at work, having to face all the different problems there. And we struggle with our relationships as much as anyone else. But I think there's a difference in that we realize that there is purpose to all of it. We realize that we are not here simply to put in our time until the dark angel calls us home to our eternal reward.

In ECK we enjoy life.

REALIZING THE PURPOSE

You wonder, *What are we doing here, going through all this misery, fighting rush-hour traffic, and elbowing people in clothing stores? What's it all about? There must be more to life.*

If the answer is "just to put in time," life doesn't make a whole lot of sense.

But some people are content with an explanation like that, I guess—if they were able to form the question, if anyone were honest enough in their religion to say, "That's all you're doing—treading water till the big day." That would be one of the most dismal aspects of a religion.

Generally, people in religions try to put their attention on the afterlife. They say, "Things will be a lot better there than they are here."

This still doesn't leave you with a very good understanding of why we're here.

In ECK, we know that we are here to go through purification as spiritual beings. This is the spiritual purification that's necessary so we can one day become a Co-worker with God.

WHAT IS A CO-WORKER WITH GOD?

Being a Co-worker with God means to work in the different levels of heaven or even here on earth, bringing divine love to people who are in need. Sometimes it's as simple as just listening to a person who's in trouble or giving something to someone in need. Or if there is a catastrophe in some part of the country, sending blankets and money.

This is being a Co-worker with God. You do this without expecting anyone to pat you on the back and say, "Well done, thou good and faithful servant."

Life doesn't often provide people to come along to pat you on the back and say something like that. But you can be the person who pats someone else on the back and says, "Hey, nice job. Glad you're here. Thanks for your help." And remembering to say "I love you" to our loved ones, because things get so fast sometimes.

We forget to be grateful for the little things.

We're so busy just with the survival of our human self that we sometimes forget to be grateful for the very dear things in our lives—our loved ones, our mates and our children, our parents, and our brothers and sisters.

We forget to be grateful for the little things.

OUR FORM OF PRAYER

In ECK, we have HU, which I call the most beautiful prayer. Our form of prayer is to sing a word—one of the holy names of God that we have learned through our initiation.

To most people, initiation means something like baptism, but instead of baptism by water, the ECK initiation is baptism with the Light and Sound of God. It's to bring Soul into a more conscious awareness of the divine love that exists, this love we all live, move, and have our being within.

This is the great love from which springs our puny human love. We do the best we can to give human love to those around us.

And some days when our tempers wear thin, when the pressures of the day have been too great, then it's just a little bit harder. We say words that we wish we hadn't uttered. We wish we could take them back, but it's too late. We've hurt someone who means a lot to us. And so then we go to them and say, "I'm sorry. I love you." If we can have the grace to do that, life goes on again, and we are just slightly better in a spiritual sense than we were before.

This word *HU* is the ancient name for God, a love song to God. I think the most apt description that I can give of it is to say that when Soul has heard this sound, Soul yearns to go home.

In ECK, we have HU, which I call the most beautiful prayer.

HUMAN LOVE, DIVINE LOVE

Soul yearns to return home to God. Home to God means the area of supreme divine love that has no conditions attached to it: unconditional love.

So often when we speak of love in a human sense, we don't see the difference. Sometimes parents say they love us, and then if we don't do things exactly their way, they'll give us the cold shoulder. Or our mate might do this, or we might do this to our mate.

Giving someone the cold shoulder is not unconditional love. It's conditional. And it's a form of control.

It's not true love at all. It's saying, "I want to do it this way, and you're not doing it my way. So until you do it my way, I'm not going to love you. I'm not going to talk to you."

Eventually the little argument blows over, and everybody is happy again and forgets until the next time.

The next time the relationship between these two people comes to a test and there is no meeting of minds and hearts, this same thing occurs. There will be some way that the two estrange each other. One of the two will give the other the cold shoulder or in some other way harm the relationship—whatever a person can do to say, "You're not doing it my way. Therefore I'm going to withhold my love from you."

It's conditional love. It's human love, not divine love. And human love is people's attempt to be godlike, whether or not they're conscious of it.

LOVE FOR SELF AND OTHERS

I think it is very important in this life to learn to love someone more than yourself—whether it's another person or a pet.

And before you can love someone else more than yourself, you begin by first loving yourself. Even Christ said, "Love thy neighbour as thyself." Right away some people think this means love your neighbor and

It is very important in this life to learn to love someone more than yourself— whether it's another person or a pet.

forget all about yourself.

Loving yourself doesn't mean to have a high, egotistical regard for yourself or go strutting around like some dictator. It means to have respect for yourself as Soul, as a child of God — or as we say in ECK, as a light of God. Because once you recognize yourself as Soul, as one of these beings of God, you've made an important step in your spiritual unfoldment.

The next important step is to know and recognize that other people are also Soul, lights of God.

Connection with the Mahanta

The ECK Masters, especially the Mahanta, the Living ECK Master, give the promise, "I am always with you." What this means is that the Holy Spirit, or the ECK, works on a personal level with every person.

The Holy Spirit, or the ECK, works on a personal level with every person.

The ECK works with each one of you who opens your heart to the teachings of ECK, the teachings of the Holy Spirit.

You have a connection with the Mahanta, this state of consciousness, this person on the inner planes we call the Inner Master. You have this connection no matter where you are, if you're at home or if you're far from home.

A woman had just finished a visit to France with her husband, and they were on their way home to Switzerland. On the way she had to go to Zurich and visit some relatives for a family celebration. Her husband wanted to go home; their daughter was waiting for them.

The husband was going to drive his wife to Zurich, then drive himself home. But it would have meant a long, long trip for him. So she finally said it would be fine if he just dropped her off at the train station.

She would make the trip to visit her relatives by herself, and he could go home and be with their daughter. So this is what they agreed to do, and she ended up at the train station.

At the same time, we were having the ECK Worldwide Seminar in Minneapolis, which is now the home of Eckankar. This woman wasn't able to go to the seminar, although many of her friends from Switzerland were going. And she wished she could be there.

She was feeling a little sorry for herself. So while she was waiting for the train, she did a spiritual exercise.

GOLDEN-TONGUED WISDOM

The Golden-tongued Wisdom is the Inner Master giving us a spiritual message.

She said to the Mahanta, the Inner Master, "If possible, please give me some assurance of your presence. Let me know that when you say, 'I am always with you,' you are really here with me."

The ECKist realized that for this to happen, she would have to look for outer signs. In other words, she would have to look at the actions and the speech of people around her and try to catch the Golden-tongued Wisdom, the Inner Master speaking through the voice and actions of other people.

The Golden-tongued Wisdom is the Inner Master giving us a spiritual message. It is part of the secret teachings for those who have the ears to hear.

If you can tune in to the Inner Master, you will find that there is such a thing as spiritual hearing and spiritual vision. It's the kind where Divine Spirit will open up truth for you so you can know something that is important to you at the time. It's usually to bring comfort, wisdom, or some form of insight or love.

So after the woman had asked the Inner Master for an assurance of his presence, she got on the train and sat down. She began to look around, paying very close attention to the people in the car, because she believed that this was how the Inner Master would make his presence known to her. And right across from her was a tall young man.

THE MAN FROM CHANHASSEN

He was just sitting there, so she didn't pay attention to him. But off to the side were two young people who had just moved to Switzerland. They were talking about their adventures living in a new country. *This must be the confirmation from the Inner Master,* the ECKist thought. She and her family had just sold their beautiful home and were thinking of moving to France or Canada or the United States.

She felt pretty sure that the Master was speaking to her through these two young people. She took out one of the ECK books, *Be the HU,* and began reading it. At one of the stops, the young couple got off the train. The woman stopped reading her book and put it on the seat beside her.

After the train was moving again, the young man seated opposite her said, "Excuse me. Do you speak English?"

For the first time, she looked at him very carefully. He had on a dark T-shirt with three sailboats on it. It was the usual kind of T-shirt you can buy in Laguna Beach or Hawaii. Except for one thing: On it, it said, "Lake Minnetonka."

Lake Minnetonka happens to be in Minnesota, very close to the Temple of ECK. And the woman happened to be on a train she had not planned to be on.

The man said to her, "Are you an ECKist?"

> This must be the confirmation from the Inner Master, *the ECKist thought.*

The woman didn't quite know what to say. She's a reserved, quiet person. The only reason he was asking, the man told her, was because he had seen her Ⓔ charm. He wasn't an ECKist himself, but he lived in Chanhassen, Minnesota. He was in Switzerland on business. In fact, he had been on the city council in Chanhassen that had determined whether or not to allow Eckankar to build the Temple of ECK. So he wanted to ask her about Eckankar.

They talked for an hour or so, and the woman came to her stop and said good-bye to the man from Minnesota.

I AM ALWAYS WITH YOU

She realized that she had gotten this confirmation from the Mahanta, the Inner Master, in a very direct way. It turned out the man from Chanhassen, Minnesota, hadn't planned to be on this train, and she had not planned to be on this train. Her thoughts were in Minnesota for the seminar, right at the area of Chanhassen and Lake Minnetonka. So who does the Inner Master—by coincidence—arrange to have seated right across from her?

And when she wouldn't notice the young man from Minnesota, he then had to say, "Do you speak English?" Make it real obvious. Wake her up.

These are the sorts of coincidences that we are very comfortable with in Eckankar. Each time they occur, it's as if a little star lights up in our life.

In ECK we often see a little blue star or blue light as a sign that the Mahanta is near.

BLUE LIGHT

In ECK we often see a little blue star or blue light as a sign that the Mahanta is near. Sometimes you'll see it in a dream or out here in everyday life.

A man went to his ophthalmologist for a peripheral vision test—to check his field of vision. This test happened to involve the use of a little flashing blue light. The light would blink on, real fast, and every time he saw one of these blue lights out of the corner of his eye, he was supposed to press a button on the test machine so the person conducting the test would know he had seen the light.

But while he was taking the test, the blue light of ECK began to shine.

At first the man didn't know the difference between the lights from the machine and the blue light of ECK. But after a while he could tell the difference. The blue light of ECK stayed on, whereas the other lights flashed and then went off.

The blue light of ECK was a star that just stayed there. And the man was afraid that the doctor was going to get a few signals in the test that really didn't fit on the record.

These experiences are just assurances of the presence of divine love. It's with an individual in the most unexpected places, one of the assurances of the reality of the Voice of God among us. The Holy Spirit is the Voice of God. And this Holy Spirit—the Voice of God—we call the ECK. It has two parts: the Light and Sound. And together, this Light and Sound are divine love.

EXPERIENCING GOD'S VOICE

We try—usually without much success—to put a name to some of the qualities of God, the divine attributes of the Holy Spirit. It's very difficult to do this with human language. In fact, it's impossible.

We can speak of divine love, and it means nothing unless you've experienced it. And we can speak of wisdom and many of these insights: seeing with the

We can speak of divine love, and it means nothing unless you've experienced it.

Third Eye, the Spiritual Eye, or hearing with the inner hearing. But people think we're speaking in metaphors—that we're using an image to try to get across an unfocused philosophy.

But we're speaking about very definite facts. We're speaking about something that actually helps us in our daily life and in the dream worlds.

For this reason alone, I would call Eckankar, the Religion of Light and Sound, the most dynamic and alive religion that exists on earth today.

I would call Eckankar, the Religion of Light and Sound, the most dynamic and alive religion that exists on earth today.

CROSSCUT OF SOCIETY

Within the ECK clergy—the ministers, the priests of ECK—we have all kinds of people. We have dynamic speakers, and we have others who are more on the quiet side.

We have fine people who act in a spiritual capacity helping those who are in trouble and need. The ECK clergy are those who have been in Eckankar for a long time and have gone through certain training that is required before they can officiate at weddings, funerals, and consecration ceremonies.

The membership of ECK is also drawn from a crosscut of society. We've all kinds of people—from the most spiritual to those who are just starting on the spiritual path. We are proud to be in association with most of them. But as in any religion, there's always one or two. One might wish they'd go off to some other religion, do their homework there, and then come to ECK when they're further along. But such is life.

MEMORIAL SERVICE

A Higher Initiate found himself in the position of assisting with a funeral for a Presbyterian family;

one of the family members had been friends with his wife for many years. The friend and her family knew about ECK, and they often sang HU, this most beautiful prayer.

They loved the sound of HU, so they sang it. But they remained Presbyterians.

One day, the friend called up and said that her mother had just died. Would he speak at the memorial service? she wondered. It would be a Presbyterian service.

The ECKist has many doubts about his own abilities to be a channel for the Holy Spirit. Although he has all these doubts and misgivings, he said, "OK, I'll do it." As soon as he hung up the phone, he turned to his wife and said, "I can't do that. It's got to be somebody closer to the family. I didn't even know her mother. They're all Presbyterians. You and I are going to be the only ECKists there. What do I say?"

His wife said, "Don't worry, dear. You'll do fine. Remember, you have this same reaction every time something like this comes up."

"Well, don't let it ever be said that in ECK there is no such thing as prayer," he said. And he sat down and prayed to the Mahanta right then.

"Tell me what to do," he asked the Mahanta. He did contemplations; he did spiritual exercises. He read the ECK books, looking frantically for anything that he could use, anything that would be appropriate for the memorial service of his wife's friend's departed mother. He found nothing.

This was Monday. The memorial service was on Wednesday. The clock was ticking, and he was frantic. When Wednesday came, he still had nothing. Nothing prepared, nothing to say. He was very nervous.

They loved the sound of HU, so they sang it.

"I can't do it. I can't go through with this memorial service." He had been saying this since Monday, thinking he could always back out at the last minute. But finally on Wednesday he decided, "I will do it. I will do it with the help of the Holy Spirit and the Mahanta." And as soon as he changed his mind, he suddenly got a feeling of confidence.

When the time came to go to the memorial service, he was ready to go. Not willing. Not eager. But ready.

HELP IN A DREAM

I have to mention one more thing that he did in preparation. When he got into a panic and couldn't find any information, he went into contemplation and asked the Mahanta, "Please let me meet with this woman and talk with her. Let me at least see her so that I will have some idea of what she is like." So the man had a dream.

In this dream, he saw a woman, the departed mother, in a kitchen. She was busy preparing food for some needy people.

The ECKist saw that she was a person who liked to give of herself to others.

The ECK High Initiate was a very quiet person. He didn't interrupt or disturb her, he just watched her running around the kitchen. She was totally happy. She was enjoying herself so completely because she was doing something for other people.

The scene shifted in his dream, and he saw her again. This time she was making toys for children, the kind of wooden toys you often saw back in the 1930s. But these toys in the dream world seemed to have power of their own. They could move back and forth and do all sorts of things.

The ECKist saw that she was a person who liked to give of herself to others. So this is all he had when he left for the church.

When he got to the memorial service, the Presbyterian son-in-law came up to him. "We'd like you to do the meditations and thoughts about the departed," he told the ECKist.

The ECKist stepped to the podium, and the words began to flow into him. He had wondered, *What did his wife's friend expect him to say?* He thought it would be the assurance there is life after death, and that their mother would be happy there. But the way his talk was forming was a little bit different.

When he got to the podium and began to speak, he spoke about Soul. He said that this woman was someone the others had loved. She was Soul. A light of God. A child of God.

She had loved to help people, the ECKist said, and she was likely doing things in the other worlds now that she enjoyed doing. He didn't get into specifics; he kept it along general lines. But he felt that the mother was very happy, that she wouldn't miss her earthly body at all. It had been ravaged by cancer. Now she was very satisfied, pleased with her new surroundings.

*She was Soul.
A light of God.
A child of God.*

LIGHT FROM WITHIN

His talk had an impact on some of the people there. Later, members of the family came up to him and talked to him about Soul being eternal, about God being love and all the things he had woven together in his talk. It had meant so much to them, they said.

After the ECKist's talk, the Presbyterian minister got up and began to give the eulogy, which the ECKist had thought he was supposed to give. But the minister ended up giving the eulogy, and the

ECKist had actually given the sermon, even though it was supposed to be the other way around.

The ECKist said he had never given a sermon in his life. But he had forgotten about all the ECK talks he had given. He just hadn't thought of them as sermons.

At the memorial service he had just been speaking to Souls, Souls who were grieving the departure of a loved one. And while he was speaking to those Souls, the life and the light of the Holy Spirit had come through him.

His wife and her friend came up to him and said that as soon as he got to the podium, a light had formed around him. His wife and her friend both noticed this separately, and they both told him. This was his experience as a vehicle for the Holy Spirit, for the Light and Sound, giving comfort to people in their time of need.

WE ARE SOUL

And this is what we try to do as we become Co-workers with God. We're practicing all the time in our daily lives, trying to be open to the Holy Spirit.

We don't tell anyone what to do or try to tell the Holy Spirit what to do. We are not directing events to fit our expectations. Not at all. We simply try to be open and aware of ourselves as Soul in the sea of other Souls as we all move through our daily work.

Whether they're photographers, writers, homemakers, or businesspeople, most people go about their work without any idea of why they're doing it. They think they're doing it for money, to make a better home for their family, to get another car or TV, or to pay off some bill. They think they're working toward some immediate goal.

We try to meet all those goals too, but we realize that behind all this, we are Soul. And the lessons of life are purifying us to make us better beings, to make us better people. To make us Co-workers with God.

EXPERIENCES ON THE INNER PLANES

Sometimes on the inner planes, I have experiences. Many of them don't lend themselves to stories to tell because they don't have a beginning, a middle, and an end.

Some of these things that happen on the inner planes are just experiences like sitting up here onstage. This is not a story. We are all just sitting here. You are listening, I am talking. That is not exactly a story unless you're going to say, "We came, we listened, we went."

When you first begin exploring the inner worlds through the elementary dream states, sometimes things are very distorted and unreal. Scenes shift and pieces don't fit together correctly. Sometimes you'll have a scene that terrifies you, then the next scene will show you as a child. And the next scene will show a totally different time period of history. Other dreams will be jumbles of images.

When people have introductory experiences in the other worlds through the dream state, they only remember a few minutes of it—for only a few minutes—before they forget.

Because it doesn't make sense out here. And if something doesn't make sense, there's kind of a churning in the stomach. The mind, rather than allow the body to suffer discomfort like this, flips a switch. It turns off the dream memory.

People don't remember their dreams because

The lessons of life are purifying us to make us better beings, to make us better people.

When people have introductory experiences in the other worlds through the dream state, they only remember a few minutes of it.

they're disjointed. They haven't learned how to travel about in their own inner worlds so that they can move from scene to scene in a way where the steps make sense, where they know exactly where they are, what they're doing, and who they are meeting there.

SOUL'S EXPANDED AWARENESS

This is part of being a Co-worker with God. When you finish the day and you go to bed to get some rest, the physical body sleeps. But as Soul, you—like everybody else who goes to sleep—leave the human body, and go out into the other worlds, and take up life there. You continue life there.

Soul is not a two- or three-dimensional being. Soul is multi-dimensional.

We measure everything here on earth by the waking and sleeping state of the human body. Therefore, we assume that when we go to sleep, we're just starting a dream.

Actually we're tapping into the expanded awareness of Soul as It is existing—as we all are existing—on the inner planes, simultaneously with our existence on the earth. It's a little hard to understand, but Soul is not a two- or three-dimensional being. Soul is multidimensional. It shares all the aspects of God. Soul can be everywhere at all times, and all places at the same time. This is that part of God that you are.

All that remains is to remember at least a little bit of this inner experience. Begin remembering your dreams to get an idea of who and what you are as Soul.

DREAM HELP IN DAILY LIFE

You'll see things; you'll gain wisdom. Sometimes you go to Temples of Golden Wisdom. Sometimes an ECK Master will be teaching you in the dream state, giving you spiritual exercises. These exercises can help you travel further into the dream worlds or get deeper insights into the secret laws of life.

In other words, you may get a better understanding of the Law of Cause and Effect—not the fact that it exists, but how it works in your everyday life. It helps you.

The dream state can help you see a cause that occurred in your life two or three weeks ago and the effect that is now showing up. You can begin to put two and two together. You realize that most of the misery or happiness that you have in your life today is what you have made for yourself. This is an important point. If you'll extend this, you'll see that nobody is a victim.

TOTAL RESPONSIBILITY

In ECK we talk about taking total responsibility for our actions. Total spiritual responsibility. I know it's a big step, but if you understand the Law of Cause and Effect, you know that something you did two weeks ago, two months ago, two years ago, or two lifetimes ago has an effect today.

Everything you do will have an effect. The seeds you plant always come back to you. Always

Everything you do will have an effect. The seeds you plant always come back to you. Always.

They come back to us in the form of poverty. They come back in the form of certain types of illness. It doesn't mean that we can't change the effects today. We can. We can go to doctors. We can work hard to get out of poverty. We can go to investment advisers. We can learn the discipline of working with money and saving, disciplining ourselves to show up at work on time so we don't get fired every other year or so. We can learn the disciplines to succeed at the things that we want to.

As we learn this cause-and-effect relationship,

we can look at the problems in our life today, trace back through the dream state or through intuition, and see how we caused today's problems in the past.

That leaves you with only one place to point the finger of blame: right back at yourself. There's only one place to start changing your future, and that's with yourself.

This is one of the places that God has designated as a testing ground for Soul.

SPIRITUAL STEW POT

Some of the ECK Masters, like Rebazar Tarzs, say this earth is the ash can of the universe. They're saying it for a reason. This is one of the places that God has designated as a testing ground for Soul.

This is the place where we all get together in a great big pot. And we try out all our anger, vindictiveness, and hatred. On the other hand, we also try out all our kindness, love, and patience.

In this pot there are people practicing a little on the negative side and people practicing a little on the positive side. All these people are mixed up in a great big stew pot. You have good people in an organization; you have bad people. Good people in a home; bad people. People who are usually good but are down today. And people who are usually down but are having a good day.

It's an incredible mix of people at all different levels of spiritual consciousness.

People of a certain kind of consciousness go off in one corner, and they call themselves Roman Catholics. Other people with a similar vision and goals go off into another corner and call themselves Buddhists. Others in other areas will be ECKists, Methodists, Lutherans, or whatever other religion exists on earth.

All of a sudden, somebody who's in this corner feels that they have outgrown this religion. So people begin to move from group to group as their spiritual needs change.

Maybe the person who's in charge of that group will say, "If you want to leave and find another place, you have my blessings." But often that isn't the case. Most often the leader will say, "Are you sure you know what you're doing? This is a very big step you're taking. It could have consequences." And you know what kind of consequences they're talking about: fire and brimstone and worse. So often, if the leaders are not of a very high ethical or spiritual nature, they will use fear to keep people within their group.

SPIRITUAL FREEDOM

I try not to do that in ECK. People come and go all the time. People come into Eckankar, and when they have gone as far as they can go, they say, "I'm going to the Methodist Church." And off they go to the Methodist Church. Then years later, they come back and say, "I went back there, and I learned a lot. Now I would like to be accepted back into ECK."

Ninety-nine percent of the time I say, "You're a lot better for the education you got in the other path. Now you know something you didn't know before."

The person may stay the rest of the time on the path of ECK, or he may not. This is how it is. We cannot hold other people in any way. Especially in ECK. We cannot do it; I will not do it. Because if I try to hold someone against their will, I am losing some of my own spiritual freedom.

It takes too much energy to keep people in Eckankar who don't want to be here. And it takes too much of my own freedom away.

We cannot hold other people in any way. Especially in ECK.

KEY EXPERIENCE

On the inner planes, I sometimes meet people who live on the Astral or the Causal Plane.

The Astral Plane is the emotional plane, the level of heaven right above the Physical Plane. The Causal Plane is the heaven right above the Astral Plane. The Causal Plane is the area of cause and effect. This is where the karmic records are stored, and if they need to see a particular incident from the past, sometimes the Inner Master takes them there to show them.

Sometimes you have an inner experience that's very important. These experiences may not come every night or every other week or twenty-five times a year. You may have one or two in your lifetime. But it's a key experience. You need it to see the significance of this life: why you found ECK.

It's a key experience. You need it to see the significance of this life: why you found ECK.

THE OLD FARMER

Even on the inner planes, they work with money and things of exchange because it's a way of expressing value. There are many areas with values similar to ours.

On the inner planes, I met an old farmer. This farmer had been farming for a long time, but his energy was running down, and so was his farm. He used to have a lot of hired hands working for him. But in the last couple of years, he was able to keep only a few. These people came and went. He'd hire some; then they'd leave because he couldn't pay them as much as he needed to.

One day, he was going to take some grain to the mill to have it ground up for the cattle. Before he left in his old truck with the grain in back, he gave instructions to the hired hands. He pointed to an old weathered barn that was full of hay bales.

"Put the bales on the wagon and drive them out to the field for the cattle," he told the hired hands.

CATTLE IN HEAVEN?

Some people are surprised at this. They say, "Cattle in heaven?" But Soul is Soul.

There's a higher consciousness growing among people on earth now.

There's a higher consciousness growing among people on earth now; they're recognizing this. Scientists are doing studies with monkeys where they seem to have a vocabulary level of a two-year-old. Dogs, in certain cases, seem to have the ability of humans to sense, perceive, and think. And still people say, "I wonder if they are Soul?" But yes, there are cattle in heaven.

The farmer drove off, and the young hands brought the wagon up to the barn. The hay bales were stacked at the back of this little barn. So instead of just carrying the hay bales through the front door of the barn, the hired hands decided, "This building is old anyway. The boards are weathered on the outside. Easiest thing to do is just take a crowbar, rip off some of these boards at the back of the barn, and move the hay bales out. That way we don't have to carry them all the way to the doorway." They thought this was very quick, very efficient. It was also very lazy and very destructive.

RESPECT FOR SELF AND OTHERS

I happened along at about this time. I saw one young hired hand take the crowbar and rip a board off the barn. I went up to him and said, "What are you doing?"

He said, "Well, I'm going to put hay bales on the wagon."

I said, "But you don't have to destroy the barn to do it."

He said, "It's an old barn."

I took him by the nape of the neck and very gently put his nose next to the board. "Don't you have any respect for this old wood?" I said.

The young hand looked at the board sort of cross-eyed because that's the only way he could look at it. Very honestly he said, "No. I don't have any respect for this old wood."

I said, "Why not?

He said, "I don't know."

And I said, "Do you want me to tell you why you don't?"

He was sincere, and he was a good person at heart. Just thoughtless. "Sure," he said.

"Because you don't have any respect for yourself."

The young man stopped a minute and thought. He didn't swing at me or anything, which was good because he would have sent me over the hay wagon and off the other side. He was bigger.

"Now listen," I said. "If you ever hire on with someone else as you have with this old farmer, use your creative powers. Use your powers to help this man restore his place. Don't destroy it with your strength."

He'd never thought of it before. He stood there just thinking about this. Finally he nodded and said, "Yeah. I see what you're saying."

In ECK, we show respect for whatever's around us— or at least we try to.

SHOWING LOVE AND GRATITUDE

In ECK, we show respect for whatever's around us—or at least we try to. We show respect for the little things that are around us, even just something like a microphone. I'm grateful for the microphone because I don't have to learn to project my voice or shout to reach to the back of the room.

And we show respect for the people we love. I'm so grateful for the people in my life who are close to me; I am so grateful that they're there.

I remember to tell them—I wish more often—that I love them. There are times we don't say "I love you" enough. If you can say this from your heart, you're showing a capability of love and respect for yourself as a spiritual being, as a child of God, as a light of God.

When the old teachers say, "Love your neighbor as yourself," you've got to start with respect for yourself before you can have respect and love for anything or anyone else. And one of the best ways to do this is to sing HU, the most beautiful prayer.

The nondirected prayer of the ECKist is the same as the one in Christianity: "Not my will, but thine be done." And in ECK, we also say, "May the blessings be."

You've got to start with respect for yourself before you can have respect and love for anything or anyone else.

ECK Springtime Seminar, San Diego, California, April 2, 1994

The man looked in my direction and asked my wife,
"What's behind the wall?" Then the curtain came down,
and the man could see. He had the most astounded look on
his face. It was priceless.

10

HU—The Most Beautiful Prayer Part 2

*T*his is the Year of Giving, our theme for the spiritual year. It's probably a good time to give someone *ECKANKAR—Ancient Wisdom for Today,* one of the introductory books that Eckankar is providing for those of you who want to give something to someone who asks about ECK. It might be helpful.

This morning I'd like to continue with a talk I began last night: part 2 of "HU—The Most Beautiful Prayer."

I was talking to my wife about it. She said, "You've said 'HU—The Most Beautiful Prayer,' but have you told what HU can do?" In other words, why sing HU?

HU, this ancient name for God, is a love song to God. You can sing it. And in singing it or holding it in your mind during times of need, it becomes a prayer. It becomes a prayer of the highest sort.

DIVINE PLAN

It becomes a nondirected prayer, which means that we're willing to let the Holy Spirit take care of

A nondirected prayer means that we're willing to let the Holy Spirit take care of the affairs in our life according to the divine plan.

183

the affairs in our life according to the divine plan instead of our personal plan.

Generally, the reason we're having problems is because our plan was fulfilled.

We have such confidence in our human mind and judgment. Sometimes there's nothing that is more of a joke than the human state of consciousness, our frame of reference. We sometimes have such a high opinion of ourselves that we even like to tell God what to do.

When doctors can't even decide what's wrong with you, it's a little bit hard if you use directed prayer. In other words, telling God what to do. For example, you have an illness and you say to God, "I need more red blood cells." Unless you really know, maybe it's wrong. Or if you're unhappy, you say, "God, I'd be a lot happier if I had more money." Maybe that's wrong too.

> *Generally, the reason we're having problems is because our plan was fulfilled.*

HUMAN CONSCIOUSNESS CONFUSION

As a person gets more experience, gets older, he begins to appreciate some of the little things of life — just being able to walk or the gift of health. Really essential things. And if other things go with it, such as wealth, that's good.

So often when we talk about sacrifice, we believe it means that we must give up everything without any regard for ourselves. This isn't quite true. It's OK to want something for yourself and your loved ones.

At a meeting last night, a man was telling me how he and his wife were trying to do something for themselves. I encouraged them. Because you can't do anything for anyone else unless you can first take care of yourself.

So many people are always out there trying to save others. I'm not talking about the good hearts who do the work quietly, who are truly becoming a Co-worker with God. I'm talking about the people who have to jump on a podium and let everybody know about this very self-righteous cause that they're backing. The cause may be to save the homeless, but these people don't do anything themselves to save the homeless except stand on a podium and blow hot air—so it's more comfortable for the homeless, I guess.

I support many of these programs for helping those less fortunate than ourselves. I'm for them, and I do what I can.

There are others who go out to Montana or Wyoming and say, "Restore this land to the natives." We're all natives if we were born here, you know. But some people are not in touch with reality. What do you do with the people who live there? Ship them to Europe? Ship others back to Africa and Asia? Just clean this place out and get it back to the way it used to be for the original Native Americans? Those original Native Americans are all gone. Times are different. What are you going to do with the land? Give it back to the buffalo? The American bison?

These people are probably living in very comfortable homes somewhere in Los Angeles or New York. I read a letter to the editor where a person said, "Why don't these people who want to save land first give New York City back to the Indians?" I thought that made a lot of sense.

With the human state of consciousness, we also see a lot of hypocrisy, but it's part of the game. We all have our own hypocrisies, but ours are OK. We just have trouble with other people's.

SETTING CAUSES INTO MOTION

We are here to do what we can to help those who are less fortunate than ourselves. But sometimes we must also remember that earth is a place for people to balance out the causes they set into motion some time ago—whether weeks, months, or years ago in this lifetime or in a past life. Many times it starts in a past life.

Each of us is an individual Soul. Each of us has set many causes into motion in the past.

These causes will have effects. If a drummer holds a drumstick and hits the drum, there's going to be an effect. There's going to be a sound. The same thing happens when we strike the drum of action in some way, at some time in our life: there's going to be a sound, a vibration from this.

We call this cause-and-effect connection karma. Sometimes it's good, sometimes it's bad.

WHICH WAY IS UP?

Generally people think of karma in terms of bad karma. But there's also good karma. In fact, there's a balance of karma; there has to be. There has to be as much good as there is bad—but not at the same time.

This is why some people are homeless and other people are wealthy. Sometimes the homeless are selfish, and sometimes they're giving. Sometimes the wealthy are selfish while others are giving. It just means that they're constantly making karma, sometimes good, sometimes bad.

Sometimes they're reaping good karma, sometimes bad karma. It all balances out. But it's a sliding scale, and it goes on and on.

We are here to do what we can to help those who are less fortunate than ourselves.

Each of us has set many causes into motion in the past.

We can get so upset about the social, political, spiritual, and religious issues that we lose our balance. We begin to do strange things like tell people to clear out of Montana when we live in New York City. And people don't like it, and they tell us they don't like it. They cause problems.

Singing HU, the most beautiful prayer, is a spiritual technique that you can use to keep your balance in this world. It can help you keep your perspective.

Sing HU. It can allow — through dream experiences, intuition, or other means — a way for the Inner Master to get through to you. The Inner Master can then let you know which way's up and which way's down — really.

Our political leaders may say, "What is up is down, and what is down is up." By chanting HU, you keep your perspective. You say, "This is the ash can of the universe, but we are here to do the best we can, to make it a garden if we can."

Keeping Our Balance

If people do things that upset us, that means that we're losing our balance. And that means we're going to do some foolish thing that's going to cost us in the end. So why do it? Why let the emotions take us over, cause us to do some stupid thing and create more karma? And it will usually be bad karma. So why do that?

When you chant HU, often the Inner Master will come to you and give you a perspective. Often the Master will say, "Hey, this stuff has been going on for centuries. And it's going to go on for centuries more."

Lord Acton said, "Power tends to corrupt and absolute power corrupts absolutely." If you recognize

If people do things that upset us, that means that we're losing our balance.

that this is part of the human condition and can accept it, if you can learn to adjust your life so that you're not always underneath the crushing wheels of power struggles, if you can do that and keep your wits when all around you others are losing theirs, then maybe you've gained spiritually in this lifetime.

These things are the realities of everyday life. These are the things that test Soul. These are the things that test you.

HU can protect. HU can give love. HU can heal. It can give peace of mind. That doesn't mean forever. It just means that if you face a crisis of some kind or another, remember to chant HU. Sing HU to yourself, or sing it out loud if no one's around.

RESOLUTIONS

One of the members of Eckankar wanted to take better care of herself, physically as well as spiritually. So she made a resolution. She decided to start doing her physical and spiritual exercises before work.

You know how resolutions are. They're very easy to make, and it's a little bit harder to keep them. But she decided that this is what she'd do.

The night before she planned to start her new schedule, she went to bed a little bit earlier so that when the alarm clock went off in the morning, she could roll out of bed and get right into her exercises.

In the morning, the alarm clock went off. The woman was in the habit of just reaching over and shutting off the alarm, then sleeping until there was just enough time to make it to work. But this time, as she shut off the alarm clock, she felt something on her hand. She opened her eyes and saw her little cat.

This is a special cat. Cats like to sleep. But this cat sleeps a lot more than most cats.

But this morning the cat didn't want to sleep. It nuzzled the woman's hand until she got up. On the second morning when the alarm went off, her other cat jumped on the bed. She didn't get up right away, so the second cat woke her up.

The ECKist knew that this was the Mahanta's way of helping her reach her objective; at that moment she didn't yet have the self-discipline to do it on her own.

Animals are Souls too.

Animals are Souls too. There's a spiritual connection that many people in our society still have to learn. Many people will never learn it. But there's a spiritual bond that connects all Souls: human, animal, and the lower forms of life.

There's a spiritual bond that connects all Souls: human, animal, and the lower forms of life.

The cats came to wake her because they caught the message. They don't communicate with words the way we do. They meow. They have their own communication if they're going to talk. Cats can talk your ear off, and they mean what they say too. Cats' meows are not just idle, aimless sounds which are just there to amuse.

ECK CURRENT

A while ago we were renting a home, and the people who owned it decided they were going to sell the place. A steady stream of prospective buyers began coming through.

Buyers were coming through the house, inspectors of one kind or another were coming through, and I was in my room trying to do my writing, preparing for talks, and answering mail. I was trying to get some work done and not be disturbed.

One day, an inspector came to look over the house. From what we'd heard from the people who owned the property, he was a very good inspector. My wife said she'd show him around.

I had two offices in that home: my desk was in one room and a double door led to a spare bedroom where I could do some of the ECK writing. I could shut the door when I wrote. Our little dog could always feel the ECK Current, the current of the Holy Spirit, coming through so strongly when I wrote. It was like a radiation burn to her. She was deaf and blind, but every time I started writing, she'd get up and walk around. We had everything covered with long strips of padding so she wouldn't hurt herself. But she'd always get up because she could feel the ECK Current coming through as I was doing the ECK writing.

My wife could feel it too; it burned her like a sunburn. So I figured the best thing to do was have two offices: a desk near where my wife worked and then right behind it a place where I could shut the doors to do my writing. Then both my wife and our little dog could handle it. Our little dog went on to doggie heaven some time ago, but my wife still feels this.

When the inspector came to the door, I thought I'd better go into my writing room and work. I left one of the doors open so that when they came upstairs to look in this room, they could just walk in.

My wife said she'd show him through our whole home first, and the last stop would be my writing room. I said, "Great."

CHANTING HU

I was chanting HU as I worked. I like to do that when others are in our home when I'm writing. It keeps the air clear so that I can write.

When the man came into the outer office with my

wife, the door to the inner room was open. I was sitting about five feet away, and it's a small room. He stood there looking. The walls were white, and the door was dark wood. And it was a big door, half open. The man looked in my direction and asked my wife, "What's behind the wall?" This is not your casual observer; this was a man who noticed details, who did inspections.

My wife was standing beside him, looking at me and wondering if this man had lost his mind. He asked again, "What's behind the wall? A walk-in closet or something?"

"No," my wife said. "A room. My husband is sitting there working—right there in the room."

Then the curtain came down, and the man could see. He had the most astounded look on his face. It was priceless. He was dazed. He walked into the room and looked around with a glazed look in his eyes, not really seeing anything anymore. I stood up and introduced myself. His handshake was limp and cold.

I just looked at him. Then I said, "You can go ahead and look around as much as you need to. Do whatever you have to."

And he said, "Yes."

The man was in hopeless shape. He walked out of the room. That was it. He was done with the inspection. No more comments. My wife just aimed him toward the front door and opened it; I got up to watch him walk out. He walked straight out the door, he made the little turn to go down the steps, and off he went to his car. He didn't look back. He didn't go fast. He didn't go slow. It wasn't an inspired walk. He was just dazed. He had no idea what had happened.

CURTAIN OF PROTECTION

The ECK had thrown up a wall, a screen. The man thought there was nothing beyond this wall because he couldn't see past the screen. This has happened other times too. I don't cause these experiences myself, but the ECK has brought it about when it was needed.

One time we were in Africa, and I was walking with a group of ECKists in a big open area. I was concerned, because most of the people were wearing robes and I was in a suit. Almost everyone was black. I thought that I'd get out there, and people would say, "Here comes a guy who's pink. There aren't a whole lot of pink people here in Africa. So that must be Harold."

But nobody saw me or my group. Except one little girl. She was real small, about four years old. The curtain that cloaked our presence only came down as far as our waists, and she was shorter than that. So she looked up at this pink man walking past.

She sees a lot of people of her own color, but she had probably never seen one of these pink strangers. *What a strange-looking person,* she probably thought. But no one else noticed us.

Other times at ECK seminars, I've gone up and down escalators and walked past people I've known for years, and they never saw me. Because at that particular moment, there was something I was on my way to do, and I didn't have time to talk. The ECK just threw a cloak around me. I find this highly amusing sometimes.

Once I was walking through a store and several people who had come in with me walked right past me. They walked past as if there was nobody there.

It would be nice to do it at will, but I don't do that.

I just put myself in the hands of Divine Spirit and let It do with me as It will.

If you say you're doing these things, then right away it gives you power over other people. People say, "Oh, I want those powers too." And I say, "Well, if you want those powers, then sing HU and raise yourself spiritually to the point where the ECK decides that you're doing something that is important enough to give you privacy for a few minutes so you can do it without anybody getting in your way."

HEALING HU

Another way that HU sometimes helps people is by healing. One of the ECK members named Heidi had a very young nephew—four years old—who hadn't seen her too often because they live in different parts of the country. The child had swallowed something and went into a coma. The doctors did everything they could, but the child was in a coma for two days.

At this point, Heidi decided she'd do something. She talked to the Inner Master, the Mahanta. "Inwardly I'm going to invite the parents and the child to sing HU with me on the inner planes if they want to," she said.

So she sat down in contemplation, and she just began to sing HU. She was careful not to make it a directed prayer, like saying, "Please, God, make this child well. Whatever's wrong, make my nephew wake up." It was nothing like that. She just did this spiritual exercise in a nondirected way: Thy will be done, not mine. Or as we say in ECK, May the blessings be.

Shortly after that, the little boy suddenly opened his eyes and saw a nurse. The first thing he said when he saw the nurse was, "Are you Heidi?"

Another way that HU sometimes helps people is by healing.

The little boy was awake and well because he and his parents had joined the ECKist on the inner planes singing HU.

WHAT CHILDREN CAN SEE

The little boy remembered the inner experience. The parents didn't, though, because as we get older, we often lose the gift of seeing the messengers or the miracles of God. They get crowded out in the rush of everyday living. They get lost through education, where the mental part of ourselves is exercised. We get better mentally, but as we do, the spiritual memories and vision fade into the background.

Children aged two, three, and four very often remember past lives.

Children aged two, three, and four very often remember past lives. But as soon as they start school, these memories begin to fade. And by the time they're six or seven, they hardly ever have past-life memories anymore. And even if they do remember and speak of them, their parents have forgotten or don't believe in such things.

When children talk about past lives, most parents think, *That child can tell stories like nobody else.* This is usually the verdict.

SING HU FOR PEACE AND SERENITY

Singing HU can also bring peace and a sense of serenity. Someone told me a story about a family that is a good example of this.

Singing HU can also bring peace and a sense of serenity.

The grandmother died. The mother was a member of ECK. Her daughter knew a little bit about ECK when she was growing up, but didn't have much use for it because of peer pressure and all this. But the daughter now had her own family.

After the grandmother died, the daughter had

trouble sleeping. Every time she'd go to bed at night, she couldn't sleep because the fear of death was so strong. And since she didn't believe in the teachings of ECK and she hadn't had any connection with them for years, she never even thought about singing HU. But she had grown up in an ECK family, and she had been exposed to the teachings of ECK.

She had come under the protection of the ECK Masters, agents of God who work in a special way with the people who they have a special affinity for or friendship with.

As she lay in bed at night, tossing and turning and trying to get to sleep, suddenly she would see this old man in her Spiritual Eye. He had long white hair and big eyes. He'd come into her room, and each time he did, the fear would leave her and she could sleep. This happened repeatedly until gradually the fear of death went away and she was able to resume her normal routines.

One day, the daughter went over to her mother's home and saw the ECK books on the bookshelf and the pictures of the ECK Masters on the wall. "That's the man who came to my room when I couldn't sleep," she said, pointing to the picture of the ECK Master Fubbi Quantz.

Fubbi Quantz served as the spiritual leader of ECK many years ago. Even though the ECK Masters who have served in this position have gone on to the other worlds, there is still a bond of love with some of the people that they have helped on the path to God in past lifetimes. Even though these people come and go from the teachings of ECK as they get what they need, the love and protection of the ECK Masters is always there if they are open to it or if there is a great need.

Even though people come and go from the teachings, the love and protection of the ECK Masters is always there if they are open to it or if there is a great need.

HU—THE MOST BEAUTIFUL PRAYER

An ECKist in Belgium had lost touch with a friend of hers. They hadn't been in contact for eight years. Then this friend wrote to her. And so the Belgian woman wrote back and told her friend how her life had changed since they'd last been in touch eight years before.

The ECKist explained that in the meantime she'd come in contact with Eckankar and she had learned this word HU, this ancient name for God, this love song to God.

She called it the most beautiful prayer.

She didn't hear from her friend again for some time. Then her friend went into the hospital for treatment for a recurring medical condition. Because of her treatments, she had to get injections for the pain every half hour throughout the night.

The friend was very frightened of the pain and the shots she needed to endure the pain. She was just terrified of having to go back to the hospital because she'd been through the painful treatments before.

But then she remembered what her Belgian friend had told her about HU, the most beautiful prayer. And she thought, *Well, there's no harm. Might as well try it. I've got nothing else facing me except this pain and fear.*

So she began to sing HU. As she sang HU, a sense of peace and calm came over her. And throughout the entire night, she didn't have any pain and didn't need any of the injections.

The next morning, her doctor asked her, "Why didn't you need any injections last night? Why were you able to pass the night in quiet sleep?"

She said, "Because of HU, the most beautiful prayer."

> As she sang HU, a sense of peace and calm came over her.

"What do you mean?"

So she explained that a friend of hers had told her about this in a letter, and she had the letter with her.

"May I read the letter?" the doctor asked.

The doctor read the letter, and he was very impressed with HU. He could see that it had the power to heal in this woman's life, so he made it part of her physical therapy. Three times a day she had to chant HU — which was quite interesting because his patient was a Catholic and wasn't in Eckankar at all.

Then the ECKist's friend had to see two other doctors. These two doctors also asked her about how she had gotten through the night without any pain. She said, "Because of this HU." And they wanted to know about it too. HU — the most beautiful prayer.

These are just examples of how to help yourself spiritually. There are many areas where HU works.

But don't expect HU to work as you want, because God's love, as it comes down and heals, does things its way. Not my will, but thine be done — the nondirected prayer. You have to have confidence and love in your heart. And you must just sing HU, for all you do.

God's love, as it comes down and heals, does things its way.

A SPECIAL SPIRITUAL EXERCISE

I would like to mention a spiritual exercise that you can do on your own at home. This exercise is simple, but it will lead you into deeper levels of your own state of consciousness.

Set aside a special time, maybe fifteen or twenty minutes a day. Try it when you're lying down in bed at night just before you drop off to sleep, or find a special time during the day that's quiet when you can sit on a couch or in an easy chair or recliner or lie down on the floor. Then chant HU. If there's a certain problem that's been facing you, if there's a certain insight that you want, or if you need the understanding to see why something is happening in your life, lightly put attention on this.

This spiritual exercise occurs quite naturally. You begin by shutting your eyes and looking into the Third Eye, the Spiritual Eye, the area just above where the eyebrows come together. You lightly put your attention there with your eyes shut.

And then begin singing HU with the question that you have in mind. For instance, Why a certain illness? Why are there certain problems at work? Why am I having such trouble with my teenage child? This sort of thing.

Sometimes it takes a day or two, or weeks, or even months, but as you chant HU, when you're deep in contemplation, all of a sudden there will be another word.

All of a sudden, you'll know that word. You may forget it afterward, but the next time you go into contemplation, you're awake again, you're conscious. You're singing HU, and after maybe fifteen or twenty minutes you'll suddenly find another word. Each one of these words—like HU or one of the secret words that come to you on the inner planes—is like a key to the secrets of God, a key to the wisdom of the divine, a key to spiritual freedom.

As you practice, this process goes much more quickly. You sit down, go into contemplation, and you sing HU. After you have practiced the exercise, the second word will come within a minute or so.

And you'll say, "Oh, that word. I always forget it. I have to try to remember it when I come out of contemplation."

If you sing that second word, it will take you to another level. It will take you far deeper into your state of consciousness than you've been before. A third word will take you to a third level. And this can even go further.

Eventually you drop off to sleep. Then you wake up, and everything is back to normal. But you will often come back with an intuitive understanding of why something in your life is the way it is. Or you will have an experience on the inner planes or inside yourself with the Light and Sound of God.

KEY TO A HAPPIER LIFE

The Light and Sound of God are the two aspects of the Holy Spirit that equal divine love. The highest form of love that you can bring into your life is through the Light and Sound. That's what we look for. And that's why we are the Religion of the Light and Sound of God.

The highest form of love that you can bring into your life is through the Light and Sound.

These are the two aspects of the Holy Spirit. And the Holy Spirit is the Voice of God. Another word we use for Holy Spirit is the ECK.

So if you want to lift yourself to a higher state of consciousness—so that the political issues, the family issues, the social issues of the day do not throw you out of balance, so that you can find a happier, more contented life while you're living here— sing HU, the most beautiful prayer.

ECK Springtime Seminar, San Diego, California, Sunday, April 3, 1994

All three people saw a giant hand grab the van just as
it was turning upside down. The hand set the van upright.

11

A GIANT HAND

A　Giant Hand refers to the Holy Spirit helping out in your life and my life in a miraculous way. Sometimes this comes in a quiet way, and sometimes it comes with a loud shout.

TREATING THE CAUSE, NOT SYMPTOMS

When Divine Spirit does something to help us, it's not simply to cure a symptom. It goes to the cause, the cause that has been lying inside you for centuries from past lives.

Today so many Western doctors are trained to treat symptoms. This is mainstream medicine, and it's very necessary and helpful in its own way. But some of the alternate ways of healing try to work with the causes of an illness.

In the same way, the Mahanta, the Living ECK Master tries to work beyond the symptoms of why a person is having a hard time in this life. The Mahanta goes back into the past and brings the problems to the front, and he gives them to the seeker of truth to work out as the seeker is able to.

When Divine Spirit does something to help us, it's not simply to cure a symptom.

GRINDING OF LIFE

What kinds of problems? Usually we talk about problems in a spiritual sense—something big such as a lack of faith, fear of life, fear of death, or no love. And when we speak of these lofty problems, those on the grand scale, we often overlook the problems of daily living.

The problems we most often encounter in life are ones like buying a new pair of shoes before the cracks in the old pair begin to look like very stylized leather. Or we run into health problems, problems on the job, problems in a relationship, or problems with losing the love of someone who is very dear to us. These are the everyday things that grind the human consciousness down into a piece of gravel and then into sand.

And out of this constant grinding of life we suddenly find we are this shining, beautiful gem called Soul.

You are Soul. You are a special being, as is your neighbor.

SOUL BECOMING GODLIKE

You are Soul. You are a special being, as is your neighbor.

Back in early Christian times, Jesus said, "Love thy neighbour as thyself." He wasn't saying that you should love yourself more than your neighbor. He said, "Love thy neighbour as thyself," because generally, Soul's evolution is such that a person first learns to love himself or herself.

Often, it's a very egotistical, selfish kind of love. At times it comes in the form of showering oneself with wealth, finery, and pretty things. These things are not bad, but sometimes this becomes the goal and the substance of living. And it is not.

The reason we're here, the reason we are like some gem hidden inside this shell of sand, being ground down, is so that we can become godlike.

This grinding by life works on the pretensions that we have, on our vanity. And gradually we become more of a light—more of a spiritual light—to ourselves and to others.

Learning to Love Yourself First

There are a surprising number of people who say, "I have to learn to love myself," almost as if it's a revelation to them. They're surprised by it. And yet they realize that the reason they treat others poorly is that they treat themselves poorly.

On the spiritual path, the first step is to love yourself.

On the spiritual path, the first step is to love yourself. After this, you grow or develop spiritually so that you can love others who are close to you—your mate, your family. Then you develop the capacity to love people beyond this narrow circle of acquaintance. You grow into a larger circle.

But the love in this larger circle that goes out beyond your close family and loved ones is a different kind of love. It's an impersonal love; it's called goodwill.

In the New Testament, the term used for it was *charity*. St. Paul spoke of faith, hope, and charity. Charity is the goodwill we offer to people outside our immediate family and friends. There's a difference between charity—goodwill—and the love we have for our close ones. We have a warm love for those who are close to us. And we certainly should have a warm love for ourselves.

Necessary Lessons

A person, a Soul, goes along the spiritual path through life getting the lessons that are necessary— whether or not the person knows they are necessary or what they're really for.

And as this process goes on, sometimes Divine Spirit, the Holy Spirit, the ECK, steps in and uses a giant hand to set things right. The ECK puts us in circumstances that normally we wouldn't have been in.

Sometimes they seem to be very good circumstances like a good job, a good relationship. Then we're very happy. But so many other times the giant hand seems to be the cruel hand of fate. It seems to be putting us with people or circumstances that we do not like. It puts us into conditions that are very painful.

And then we cry to God. We say, "God, help me. Save me from this evil."

But in ECK, we know that this hand of evil is our own hand reaching from back through the centuries. And the evil that we face in this lifetime, the evil that we face today, is simply payment for the past. Some deed, some thought from the past needs repayment. And this is what we call karma.

Who are you? Where have you been? And what does this life mean with all the different experiences that come your way?

That's all karma is. That's the bad karma. The good karma is the blessings that come into our life. They do not simply happen. They happen for a reason. They happen be*cause*. That nice little word, *cause*.

So the Mahanta, the Living ECK Master deals with causes. He helps you through dreams, through Soul Travel, and in other ways to truly look at yourself.

To look at yourself. Who are you? Where have you been? And what does this life mean with all the different experiences that come your way?

Film Savings

Sometimes the giant hand of Spirit works in very small ways. It makes things right.

A college student in New York City went into a store to have some film developed. The clerk told him, "When you pick up the film, it's going to cost this amount. But if you pay right now, you can save 10 percent." That was $1.25.

The student didn't have the money on him. And the automated teller machine was several blocks away. Plus he would have had to run all the way to the teller machine, run all the way back, and get in a long line again.

A dollar twenty-five, he thought. *It will take me that much time and energy to go there and come back. According to the Law of Economy, it's just not worth it.*

Being a student, he was very much aware of the dollars and cents. So he said to the clerk, "I'll pay when I pick up the film."

He was going to go home on the subway, and as he got to one of the gates that allow passage into the subway, he noticed the gate was broken. The attendant said, "This will be down for five minutes. So you can just go through."

The student found it very interesting that the amount he saved was $1.25.

Dodge Acclaim

At other times, this giant hand comes to put a check on our pride. A mother was feeling very good because she had been giving her son's baseball team some instruction on how to bat. On this particular evening, she was filled with the day and she'd been bragging with her coworkers about the batting practice, making a nuisance of herself.

She was seeing headlines; she imagined her name in great flashing lights on some kind of a marquee: *So and so, trainer of great baseball stars when they were young boys.*

As she drove into the parking lot of the restaurant where she and her family were going to have dinner, the mother saw a car just like her own. She had a Plymouth Acclaim. This car, which looked just like her car, had "Dodge Acclaim" written on the back.

"Dodge doesn't make that particular model," she said to her family. "Dodge makes the Spirit, which is just like the Plymouth Acclaim, but Dodge does not make an Acclaim."

She looked at it again. "Dodge Acclaim. How can that be? There isn't such a thing," she said again. "Somebody must have goofed and put Dodge on the sign when they meant to put Plymouth."

Then she realized that the message was for her: *dodge acclaim, avoid praise.*

When we first try to be spiritual, we stumble a lot of the time.

She understood that whatever she was doing to help her son's baseball team, no matter how good they got, her service was to be a quiet act of love.

When we first try to be spiritual, we stumble a lot of the time. She caught herself quickly because she was further along on this spiritual path. As soon as she saw the Dodge Acclaim, she realized the message was to avoid acclaim, avoid the praise of other people.

Because if you're doing anything for the praise of others, you're not doing it for God. You're not doing it for love. And if it's not for love, then it's for nothing.

SEEING OUR ANCIENT PAST

I use the terms *ECK* and *Eckankar* interchangeably sometimes. Eckankar refers to the spiritual path out here. ECK refers to the eternal teachings which have existed even before people began to speak and communicate with each other. The ECK Masters in the ancient times taught through the dream state. People had dreams, visions, and other insights— intuition—about where danger was.

Spiritual guidance was with primitive mankind from the very beginning. When I refer to primitive mankind, I'm referring to you in a long-ago life.

We read about the Iceman, this man who was found up in the mountains between Austria and Italy near Switzerland. He was very well preserved, and people thought he was some poor traveler who had perished up there last winter. They didn't realize he was maybe five thousand years old.

When we read the history of primitive mankind, we generally say, "This is about somebody else, way back then. How dull." But for those of you who are fortunate to work with your dreams, sometimes the Mahanta, the Living ECK Master opens you up to past lives. You begin to see these past lives in the dream state or through Soul Travel and you see the lesson that past life was bringing through.

You begin to understand the main things that life brought for you to learn.

You see what you spent that whole life learning. You begin to understand the main things that life brought for you to learn.

WHAT WE SPENT LIVES LEARNING

You may have learned how to show compassion to others, simply because in a previous life you had no compassion for others. Sometimes you were the torturer; sometimes you were the tortured. Some-times the king, sometimes the slave.

Each of your past lifetimes taught you at least one particular lesson and sometimes more.

Of course, there were other lifetimes that were pretty bland. These were the ones where there were no great lessons, and it was simply a time of healing. Sometimes between very strenuous lifetimes, people come back just to heal. They end up in a quiet lifetime in a pastoral setting of some sort.

HU is an old name for God, and if you sing it, it's a love song to God.

LIFE IS A SERIES OF STEPS

HU is an old name for God, and if you sing it, it's a love song to God. It's a very simple song, but if you're in trouble, in pain, in need of comfort, or in need of love, sing HU quietly to yourself. This is practically the only gift I can give you.

If you know how to sing HU, you can open yourself to the Holy Spirit. You can open yourself to the help that It's offering you to help you take the next step.

Life is a series of steps. We go from one step to another, from one lifetime to another. Sometimes the moment is very exciting and exhausting—whether the moment is a lifetime or an hour. Another time, it may be a very pleasant and soothing time, a time for reflection and contemplation, so that we have a chance to look around, to look back, to look forward— to see what truth is in our lives.

This searching, this time of quiet reflection or contemplation, also awakens the desire for more truth. It will awaken a stronger desire for God—a stronger desire for love.

Generally, what drives us to look for this love is pain, trouble, and all the things that we believe make this life very difficult to bear. These are actually the things that drive us to the spiritual path. The troubles of the body are the joys of Soul.

THE SUBSTITUTE TEACHER

Sometimes, the Holy Spirit uses people, like the teacher in this next story, to tell others about HU.

A teacher had a friend who was a substitute teacher staying in her guest room. Later when the friend came out of the shower, she said, "The heater in your bathroom makes a very interesting sound."

The ECKist said, "What do you mean?"

The friend said, "Oh, it's just a very interesting sound."

The ECKist said, "You mean like HU?"

"Yes, exactly."

The ECKist said, "That's probably because every time I shower, I play my audiocassette *HU: A Love Song to God*."

The next night, the friend was using the bathroom to clean up. When she came out she said, "You know, I heard the HU again. But what are the musical instruments that back up the HU?"

As you know, there aren't any musical instruments recorded on that audiocassette of the HU Song.

The ECKist knew that as her friend was hearing the HU with her inner ears, she was opening up her state of consciousness to the higher planes. She was hearing the sounds of God at higher levels.

She was hearing the sounds of God at higher levels.

"What instruments are playing in the background when you're listening to the HU?" the ECKist asked her friend. And her friend told her.

That gave the ECKist an opening to speak about the different sounds of God that occur at different levels—the tinkling of bells and some of the more common sounds that occur on the different planes of God. Sometimes a person will hear a very high whistle. I heard that for a number of years after I'd come into ECK. It was a very, very high whistle. Sometimes it's a chorus of voices, like medieval monks chanting. Other times it's the song of a bird, and you think you're actually hearing a bird singing in the night, but it's the song of a bird that doesn't sing at night.

The friend was hearing these different sounds as she listened to the HU, not understanding that these were actually the sounds of God coming from within herself.

When you hear this music of God, it purifies and uplifts you spiritually.

When you hear this music of God, it purifies and uplifts you spiritually. This is why it's important. It burns off some of the karma that you've created in the past, and it prepares you to accept a new spiritual step in your life.

HEALING THE HEART

Another woman had gone to some ECK introductory lectures, and she learned about chanting HU. But she didn't know how to do it right.

Somebody had just told her, "If you're in trouble, say HU." But they didn't demonstrate how to sing it. So the best she knew how to do was say, "HU HU HU HU HU," over and over. That's what she had figured out.

This woman had a heart condition that had become more serious, but she had no fear of life, which I find interesting. Usually you say a person was not afraid of death, but this woman wasn't afraid of life. She had had three heart attacks, each one more serious than the last.

During the third one, the doctors thought they would lose her.

But while she was semiconscious and the doctors were trying to revive her, she remembered this word *HU*. She had just heard about it and didn't know how to sing it, so she began to say, "HU HU HU HU HU," quietly inside herself.And suddenly on the monitors, the doctors saw her vital signs coming back to normal, one after another.

When she opened her eyes, one of the doctors said, "What are you doing? Whatever it is, stop. We've got enough complications. Otherwise we can't prescribe you a drug."

And she said, "Please don't disturb me. I'm singing HU."

AT THE HAIR SALON

Sometimes this giant hand touches you, and suddenly, on the spur of the moment, you have to do something.

After work one night, an ECKist suddenly decided to go to have her hair cut. It was a spur-of-the-moment decision, so she went to a salon where you just go in and sign up, then wait for a stylist to be free. It's a place for people who have very busy lifestyles.

The last few times this ECKist had gone there, she had gotten a certain stylist. So instead of taking just anyone this time, she asked for that particular woman.

But she had to wait much longer than usual. She saw other customers coming in the door, sitting down, then going into the back to have their hair cut. They'd come out, but she was still seated there.

She began to wonder what was taking so long. She had a letter to mail. Should she get up now, run out quickly, and try to mail the letter? She didn't want to lose her place in line. Probably the moment she ran out to the mailbox, her hairstylist would come out. And if she wasn't there, somebody else would get her place in line.

After about forty-five minutes, her hairstylist came out, apologized for running late, sat her down and put the cape on her, and began to work on her hair. Suddenly a teenage boy ran in the salon. He called the stylist over, and the ECKist could see them talking very excitedly, as if they were agitated about something.

When the hairstylist came back to her chair, she said, "The best friend of my son was just killed in an accident."

The ECKist said, "If you want to leave, don't worry about my hair. I can always come back some other time."

The stylist said, "No, if I don't go on now, I'm just going to lose it."

She was fighting her emotions, trying to deal with this very difficult problem that had just come into her life. She knew her son's best friend. And she was trying to come to grips with his death.

As she did the ECKist's hair, they began to talk about life in general. The ECKist just listened, never mentioned anything about the ECK teachings. She just listened because here was another Soul in a moment of grief, in a moment of agony, needing to talk the grief out.

After her haircut was finished, the ECKist got up to go. They hadn't exchanged one word about Eckankar, but the stylist felt better than she had before.

WE WORK FOR GOD

Nearly always, when Divine Spirit puts you in an area where someone else is speaking of their heartache, you are there as a vehicle for the Holy Spirit. The Holy Spirit reaches out to that person through you, another human being. Because often the only way people can accept the love and the help of Divine Spirit is through another human being.

So when you make yourself available at times like this—at critical times in other people's lives, at a crossroads—you are being a worker for God, a giant hand.

God often works through us. We are small and insignificant, perhaps, when seen in the light of the masses of people that exist on earth. But if you look at this in a different light, you see that all the individuals in this mass of humanity are lights of different brightness. Some of them going through hard times when they need your help. They need your listening ear. If we can see it this way, we can understand how God works through us and we can grow spiritually ourselves.

As we come farther on the path of ECK, we realize that our purpose for being here is not just to live long enough so that we can die and go to heaven. What's living for? If it's only to put in time—to live to some artificial standard age, to be ready for that last great day—we've wasted our life. If we don't do anything to be there for others when they need us, we've really wasted our lifetime.

The Holy Spirit reaches out to that person through you, another human being.

We can understand how God works through us and we can grow spiritually ourselves.

A TRULY SPIRITUAL PERSON

In the small country church where I grew up, there were those people who were truly spiritual.

Every organization has its truly spiritual people. They're usually the ones who are helping others— but not if the others don't want help.

You don't want people coming to your door, trying to twist your arm to become a member of their faith. When I say truly spiritual people, I'm not talking about the people who do that. Often those are not very spiritual people, I'm afraid.

If you say, "No, thank you. I have my own religion. I'm very happy with it," and if the people say, "I'm very happy for you," and walk away, that's a sign of a highly spiritual person. But if the person tries to argue with you and convince you that you're wrong in your understanding of God, that's a very good sign of a person who is not very far along on the spiritual path.

FACING YOURSELF

I know this is shocking. When it's our religion, we think the missionary work is good and all the missionaries are good people.

But even in ECK, we have those people who know how to let others have their beliefs and validate them. And there are other people who try to push the ECK teachings on others who don't want them.

The same is true in the different denominations of Christianity. There are those who understand spiritual freedom and those who do not. There are those who understand spiritual love and those who don't. It's like the old saying in the Bible: "By their fruits ye shall know them."

Of course, it's always other people, not ourselves, who carry a big banner that says, "I'm narrow-minded." Of course, we don't. Others carry big banners that say, "I'm a bigot." Of course, we don't. Others carry big banners that say, "I am thoughtless, and I don't care about you or your beliefs." Of course, we know better. We're not that way.

I can guarantee you that if you have any of these vanities—which are very natural for the human condition—you're going to have to come face-to-face with them in time on the path of ECK. In the ECK teachings, you're going to have to come face-to-face with yourself, usually sooner than later. For this reason, I call the path of ECK a vibrant path.

The dynamics of the path of ECK are such that your thoughts and your actions come back to you in quick order.

The dynamics of the path of ECK are such that your thoughts and your actions come back to you in quick order.

People in other paths or faiths haven't always made a commitment to face themselves.

They have a lack of love toward themselves that comes out in how they treat others. And this has an effect spiritually. But the effect generally doesn't have to occur immediately if there's no commitment to face themselves. In ECK, however, this path brings the possibility of spiritual freedom in this lifetime.

And because of that possibility, the Mahanta, the Living ECK Master helps you by bringing you the effect of the causes you set into motion. He allows these to come back to you almost immediately.

This path brings the possibility of spiritual freedom in this lifetime.

Pretty soon, you learn that if you're on the path of ECK, it takes a real dummy not to see the problems you've caused for yourself. Because they come so quick. A harsh word comes back very quickly.

Truth Telling

An ECKist was at work, and he heard a funny story that made fun of another employee. He thought this would be a very, very funny story to tell a fellow worker.

They went out to lunch at a Chinese restaurant, and he had just leaned over to whisper the story to his friend as they were opening their fortune cookies.

His fortune said, "If you need to whisper it, don't say it."

This is the giant hand of Divine Spirit, working through the Mahanta, the Living ECK Master. Those of you who become members of ECK have turned your inner spiritual affairs over to a higher power, saying, "Show me thy ways, show me the truth."

And you begin to learn the truth. First you learn the truth about yourself, and sometimes it can be a very painful truth because you see yourself as others see you. It can be an eye-opening experience.

We have images of how we appear to others — not just physically, but in our dealings with others. We think certain people like us and respect us, and then perhaps when we're in ECK, we overhear the whisperings of what other people we work with actually think about us. It's a sobering thought, especially if it's true.

PREVIEWS

Sometimes the Mahanta, the Living ECK Master will give a preview to an ECK initiate. "Tomorrow," he'll say, "something's going to happen in your life, so be ready."

An ECK initiate woke up one morning and told his wife, "I had this dream. It doesn't make any sense to me." He worked in a gas company, and he had many different jobs, one of which was to light the gas lanterns that some people have on their lawns. They go out, and he has to go to their homes and start the lanterns again. In the dream, the man went out to someone's house with his wife and started the lantern.

His wife said, "Well, what else?"

He said, "That's it. That was the whole dream."

Dreams are close. They give you a hint. His wife didn't quite understand the dream either, but she said, "Maybe it means that Divine Spirit wants us to go out there and give people news of the Light of God."

When he went to work that day, he was asked to do some kind of repair on a gas line, not on a lamp itself. As he was working on the gas line in the yard of a residence, a little boy, about preschool age, came up to him.

Out of the blue the boy asked, "Are you the Master?"

Out of the blue the boy asked, "Are you the Master?"

The ECKist didn't quite know what to say. First he tried to ignore the question, thinking to himself, *What does that kid mean? Does he mean like a master carpenter or a master in some trade?*

But the boy asked the same question a couple more times. He wouldn't quit. "Are you the Master?" he repeated.

ARE YOU THE MASTER?

As the little boy was asking, "Are you the Master?" the man from the gas company said, "I'm not. Why do you ask?"

"Who is the Master?" the boy asked.

So now the man's got another problem. He wants to tell the little boy about Eckankar because the boy's asking a very direct question.

Many of the children who are coming into the world today have come here ready for Eckankar.

Many of the children who are coming into the world today have come here ready for Eckankar. That's why they came back. And that's why this little boy was asking.

But this man was being very respectful of the child's religion. He did not want to have the parents feel that he was telling the child about another religion when it wasn't the correct thing to do. In a family, children are learning a certain set of spiritual, moral, and ethical guidelines. You don't want to confuse them by having other people preach words into their head. If a parent is going to be at all successful in teaching the spiritual, ethical, or moral guidelines to a child, it's going to have to be done not just through words but through actual behavior. A child can see what the parent is like. When there's a poor role model, the child stands a good chance of becoming just like the parent because children do what they see.

So the man just said, "If you want to know who the Master is, chant HU. Just sing HU." That's all he could say, and he showed the young boy how to sing HU.

The boy seemed satisfied. Just then, some other children ran up and then everything was back to normal. Kids playing. And the man finished his work and left.

Seeing Soul's Light

Children before age five, six, or seven can still see the Light of God, this light of Soul, that's around people. Until she was four or so, my daughter could see the same thing. When she was in kindergarten, I asked her, "Can you see lights around people?"

"Yes," she said.

"What colors do you see?" I asked.

She mentioned different colors, some she liked and others she didn't. "When do you watch these lights?" I asked her.

"Usually when the parents come to pick their kids up."

"Well, where do you stand?"

She said, "I just stand against the wall in the school, and I just watch them." And I could just imagine this little kid, standing along the wall watching parents pick up their children. She mentioned certain lights she liked—the bright, clear ones—and the murky, dark ones she didn't like. She kept away from those people. Here was this little kid, four years old at the time, just observing the lights in people.

She made quite a study of it. Every day, I'd ask her, "Well, what lights did you see today?" But as she got older, it stopped.

As children get older, the materialism in the classroom and having to fight off drugs and violence, causes the Spiritual Eye to shut. Usually it stays shut for years until they come in contact with the ECK teachings again. Or, in her case, it transferred into seeing in other ways—through the dream state and other areas where she gets her spiritual insights.

If you want to know about their past lives, ask them, "What did you do when you were big?"

You have to know how to talk to very young children. If you want to know about their past lives, you have to ask them questions like, "What did you do when you were big?" In other words, when they were an adult. You have to talk the way children in this lifetime understand. Because parents often don't know how to do this, they lose out on some of the richest insights into spirituality that are available to them. And these insights come right through their own children.

Don't pry, though. Sometimes children don't care to talk about past lives. Sometimes they want to talk about them for two or three minutes, and then they're

done. They want to get up and play; they want to do
something else. So don't subdue them because you're
bigger; don't say, "No, I want to hear more. Tell me
more."

A GIANT HAND

A woman in Wyoming had had several back op-
erations, making it very difficult for her to move
around. But one day, she had to go out of state with
a friend to pick up a load of pallets in a van with a
trailer attached.

The men stacked the pallets on the trailer, but
they didn't do a very good job. As the ECKist's friend
drove back to Wyoming, the ECKist noticed that the
trailer swung back and forth, making the driving
very unsteady.

"It's hard steering, isn't it?" she said. And she
offered to drive to give her friend a rest.

The ECKist got behind the wheel, and they took
off down the road. As they were crossing a bridge,
suddenly the trailer began to sway more and more.
The van and the trailer swung around in opposite
directions. Then they headed straight down into a
deep ditch.

The ECKist remembered seeing the ground coming up very fast, as the van began to flip.

And then suddenly, everything righted itself. The
van was still in the ditch, but it was upright.

A state trooper came on the scene and interviewed witnesses to the accident. Several people had
stopped. Witnesses in different cars, who hadn't
talked with each other, all said the same thing,
the trooper told the two women.

"All three people saw a giant hand grab the van
just as it was turning upside down. The hand set the

van upright," he said. "I can't report this. How can I put this in my report? A giant hand turned a van right side up so that it didn't fall on its roof?" The state trooper walked back and forth, trying to figure out how to write a report that wouldn't make him the laughing stock at headquarters.

This is just another example of Divine Spirit intervening in the lives of those people who have a spiritual reason to have the protection of the Mahanta, the Living ECK Master.

Put your attention on your dreams tonight if you want to. I won't give you a special spiritual exercise. There are plenty of them around. They are seeds of contemplation. In *Stories to Help You See God in Your Life,* ECK Parables, Book 4, there are little contemplation seeds throughout.

Watch your dreams, and in the morning see if there's a spiritual lesson coming through from the Inner Master just for you.

If you have the book, find something in it that catches your fancy. And when you go to sleep, think lightly about it. Don't belabor it. Don't make it a heavy thing. But watch your dreams, and in the morning see if there's a spiritual lesson coming through from the Inner Master just for you.

ECK Summer Festival, Minneapolis, Minnesota, Saturday, July 2, 1994

The most important experiences were the ones that let me go from Japan, where I was stationed with the Air Force, back home to the farm in Wisconsin. The experiences proved to me that there was a continuity in life that distance could not cut in two, like a scissors cutting a string.

12
JUST KEEP
MOVING AHEAD

*T*he ECK youth were going around asking some of you questions, and maybe they were the same ones I have here. They asked if they could meet with me, but the schedule was full. So my secretary asked them, "If you had a chance to ask Harold a question, what would you ask?" They came up with three questions, and the questions are quite good.

BALANCING THE SCALES OF LIFE

The first one is What are your joys of being in Eckankar?

My joys of being in Eckankar are simply gratitude for the chance to let other people hear about the Light and Sound of God. It's that simple. My joy doesn't come in saying, "If you join Eckankar, your life is going to be a bed of roses," because I can't say that.

As many of you realize, when you come into Eckankar, your life suddenly takes on direction. I don't know how to say it better.

Life takes on direction. It has purpose. It has a

My joys of being in Eckankar are simply gratitude for the chance to let other people hear about the Light and Sound of God.

spiritual purpose, probably more of a purpose than you have ever experienced before. Sometimes this means having to balance the scales of your life, wherever you have tipped them sometime before.

When we tip the scales of life, sometimes we tip them in our favor and sometimes we tip them against ourselves. But when you come to Eckankar and begin with the teachings of Light and Sound, your life is going to take a new direction.

PERSONAL RESPONSIBILITY

It will be a very straightforward and definite direction. Your life will become one of personal responsibility.

A very good article about Eckankar appeared in the Minneapolis paper yesterday. One point that they didn't understand was about spiritual law.

Your life will become one of personal responsibility.

The reporter said we don't have a very defined code of ethics. But the spiritual law is very definite. I've been trying to bring you a code of conduct in the very simplest way I know. These are Richard Maybury's two laws. They are two simple laws discovered by someone who is not a member of Eckankar: "Do all you have agreed to do," and "Do not encroach on other persons or their property."

AN OPEN-ENDED PATH

Question two from the youth: Who influenced you the most in becoming an ECK Master?

Without a question it was Paul Twitchell, the modern-day founder of Eckankar. He was the greatest influence for me in following the path of ECK.

Until then, I had been having experiences that I couldn't explain. When I read his books, I said, "This sounds as good as anything I've heard." I had joined a number of other organizations at about the same time, but after I had gone through the others, I saw where they all came to a dead end.

The path of ECK was an open-ended path, and so I continued with it. And my greatest influence was definitely Paul Twitchell.

HU EXPERIENCE

The third question was What was an important experience you had from singing the HU?

There are so many.

When I was first in ECK, I didn't really understand that all sounds come from HU. So I would sing any number of the different sounds of God that occur in the different planes. But some of the most significant experiences came when I sang HU.

The most important experiences were the ones that let me go from Japan, where I was stationed with the Air Force, back home to the farm in Wisconsin. I was very homesick at the time. The experiences proved to me that there was a continuity in life that distance could not cut in two, like a scissors cutting a string.

To me, this was very important. I had a strong love for my family, and I was separated from them by many miles.

In an indirect way, these Soul Travel experiences were what allowed me to fulfill the love I felt for my family. And I didn't realize that for years. So the experience was with Soul Travel, but the important part of that experience was having divine love and having the chance to fulfill it through seeing my parents and being home on the farm on several occasions.

In an indirect way, these Soul Travel experiences were what allowed me to fulfill the love I felt for my family.

JUST KEEP MOVING AHEAD

An initiate I talked with several years ago was having a problem listening to the problems of ECK initiates who were having problems with other ECK initiates. And the person wondered what to do, how to deal with this.

At the time, I said, "Just keep moving ahead."

I was trying to say that if other people are going to go off on sidetracks, if they're going to wander around in cul-de-sacs, dead ends, and things like this, let them. Because they need the experiences. But this person was earnest and wanted to move forward spiritually. So the answer was Just keep moving ahead.

Once a person becomes a member of Eckankar, he or she finds that suddenly there is a very direct course that life takes for them. Before, you were sailing a ship without a rudder or a sail. At first, it seems as if someone put a sail on your boat, and you're sailing fast across the water. And you say, "This is great."

Later, you realize there is a rudder on this sailing vessel too.

Then you realize that you're the one who has to go back and hold the tiller. Otherwise, you've got speed, but where are you going?

You're almost worse off than before, unless you do the Spiritual Exercises of ECK. They give you the wisdom to read the stars, if you will, to find out and know where you are. Then you can decide where you want to go and steer a course. Unless you do the spiritual exercises, you're going to end up on the rocks.

Just keep moving ahead.

Just keep moving ahead.

ECK SATSANG SURPRISE

A group of ECKists were meeting in a private home for Satsang class, studying the spiritual teachings of ECK. I write a series of discourses, or letters, and as a member of ECK, you get one a month. We have *The Easy Way Discourses* and *The Dream 1 Discourses* that come with the first years of membership. People get together and discuss and study the discourse lessons, learn from the spiritual exercises in them, and have a whole month to work on this in the privacy of their own homes.

This group of ECKists had just finished the class when there was a knock on the front door. "No one ever uses our front door," the Arahata said. "Everybody comes through the side door."

But a woman was at the door. And she didn't know how to explain why she was there and why she was knocking. She said that she had inner guidance that something very spiritual was going on in this town. She lived thirty miles away. Her inner guidance told her to get in her car and just drive, and when she got to this certain area, she'd know.

The ECK, Divine Spirit, doesn't send people off on wild-goose chases. So this was the first house she'd come to.

The ECKist said, "We're having an ECK Satsang class. You're welcome to come in." And so she came in. Her inner guide had brought her right to this home, right to an ECK Satsang class.

The ECKists there told her some basic things about Eckankar and gave her some brochures. Later she went home. She just kept moving ahead. She got the guidance, and she followed it. It's now up to her to do what she wants with this opening of the door.

She got the guidance, and she followed it. It's now up to her to do what she wants with this opening of the door.

INNER GUIDANCE AND
THE SOCIAL CONSCIOUSNESS

Often people are afraid to follow their inner guidance. It sounds like such a foolish thing to do, especially if they have to face other people and explain why they are doing what they are doing.

One of the very strong pressures in a seeker's life is the social consciousness: What will people think? What will people say?

The social consciousness is so strong that it keeps people in religions that they have outgrown years ago.

The social consciousness is so strong that it keeps people in religions that they have outgrown years ago. But they're afraid to leave because they worry about what the neighbors will say. It is a very strong force that the negative power uses to keep people in line.

It keeps them trapped in their present life, in their state of futility, in their state of hopelessness and unhappiness. Most people do not have the spiritual strength to muster the courage to take a step away from the crowd.

YOUR NEXT STEP

Most of you just didn't fit in with the groups you were in before ECK. You said, "There has to be more to life than what I have now."

These forces in life—pain, unhappiness, joys—were the motivating factors, and you came to ECK. The Mahanta or the ECK used these factors to bring you to your next step.

People come to ECK and stay here for a while. And after a while they may have gotten as much as they can take in this lifetime. Perhaps they just came for an introductory tour. So after a few years, they may say, "I've gotten as much from the path of ECK as I can. I want to go back to my other religion." Or they follow some other teaching for a while.

It's perfectly all right with me. If someone is ready for ECK, they'll want to be in Eckankar.

If they feel that it's not right for them, it means that their inner direction is showing them a need to move somewhere else. It's telling them to go to some other teaching to fill in their spiritual understanding.

Once they've plugged the holes and filled in the potholes in their pathway to God, they'll come back to the path of ECK.

ARRANGED KARMA

But until they make the choice, until they choose to come back, it's their business and their business alone. It's not for me to tell them, "If you leave the path of ECK, you're going to have all these trials and hardships." It may happen. In fact it often does. But I don't tell people that.

It happens for a very simple reason: When someone first comes to the path of ECK, the Mahanta, the Living ECK Master takes over the karma for this individual. He arranges it, puts it in neat little rows, and then gives it back.

People must pay their own debts. They must reap their own rewards.

People must pay their own debts. They must reap their own rewards. I can't do that for them. No one can do it for them. In ECK, we don't have the concept of a savior, because we're not saving anybody from anything—unless we're helping people save themselves from themselves.

This is what karma is: doing it to yourself, and then complaining about others doing it to you.

WAYS GOD SPEAKS TO SOUL

An important facet of the ECK teachings is the study of dreams. There are a number of ways that God speaks to people.

God can speak to us directly through the Sound or Light. Sometimes in contemplation or during your day you'll see a blue or white light. Know that this is the presence of God. It's the presence of God that's come to uplift you spiritually, to purify your heart, to make you ready for the next step on your journey into the heart of divine love and mercy.

Sometimes God speaks through the Sound, and It can be the sound of a musical instrument. It can be one instrument or a number of instruments playing together. It can be the sound of a storm. It can be the sound of thunder. It can be the sound of a drum. It can be the sound of a bird singing. Sometimes It can be the sound of a soft sigh. It can be almost any sound. But if It leaves you uplifted, with a feeling of goodness and love, then you can be assured that this is one of the blessings of God. It was the Voice of God come to uplift you spiritually.

DREAMS ARE IMPORTANT

A more concrete way we hear God speaking is through dreams. But dreams are more indirect, because dreams work through experiences in the other worlds seen as through a dark cloud.

Often people must learn to interpret their dreams. These experiences you're having in the higher worlds, the higher heavens, are clouded by illusion. This is another one of the tricks of the trade of the negative power we call the Kal. You can call it Satan or the devil; it doesn't matter. Its purpose is to trick and mislead you so that you never really see the importance of dreams, for example. So that you say, "Dreams aren't important."

But I say, "Dreams are important. They are one of the ways that God speaks to you."

It's up to you to learn how to interpret your own dreams. Why should you listen to someone else interpret your dreams? I do it sometimes for people if they want to know what this or that means, but I do it very seldom. Because it's the lazy person's way out.

Dreams are important. They are one of the ways that God speaks to you.

Rule of Life

The social consciousness is in the habit of having other people answer the questions. People always want some other authority to come into their life and make things right. Why? Because people are trained to be irresponsible. If something goes wrong anywhere in life, right away they say, "I am a victim."

Accidents do occur here and there which are karmic return, and sometimes someone else has started it. They start the roll of karma by initiating an act which you then respond to.

You respond either with an open heart — without reacting to it — or, in most cases, you respond with some kind of reaction like anger. You shoot back a response. One thing leads to another, and then you come to blows —if not physically, then emotionally or mentally.

All these little blows have to be smoothed over, patted down, and paid off. This is karma. It's a very simple rule of life.

PATH OF TOTAL RESPONSIBILITY

Once you come to the path of ECK, you can look at these instances where you have broken the spiritual law. The payment comes so quickly that you know, *I am paying for this deed myself.* You know this even though life or the Holy Spirit has seen fit to make the experience come at the hands of another person. You can say, "I caused this myself."

Thus the path of ECK is the path of total responsibility. There's no excuse for saying, "I am in this condition because of factors beyond my control."

Too many people started out in the same position and have made a success of themselves. That excuse really doesn't hold up.

If you're really sincere about moving forward in any number of different ways—financially, emotionally, mentally, in your education, or spiritually—that excuse no longer works. Because others have done it. Others have pulled themselves up by their bootstraps. People in much worse conditions have succeeded. And if they have, so can you.

The payment comes so quickly that you know, I am paying for this deed myself.

BUILDING A STRONG SPIRITUAL FOUNDATION

An ECKist had a series of very good dreams that told about his spiritual life. The dreams came years apart.

In the first dream, he saw a foundation being laid for a building. But it wasn't put together very well, and this first building was destroyed. The whole thing fell down.

This was showing his life before ECK. It was teaching him certain basic rules of how to live with other people, how to respect life, and how to respect other people's property. What we were referring to before in Maybury's two laws. This was good, and he saw this in his dream. A house that is not built well collapses in upon itself.

After coming into ECK, the man had another dream. And in this dream, he saw the concrete foundation being laid for an incredibly large building. He realized that this huge concrete foundation represented the teachings of ECK, and he could only imagine what kind of building would go on top of the foundation. He knew it was the temple of his own being.

Sometime later another dream came to the man. This time he saw the same concrete foundation, and now a framework of steel was going up on top of it.

This building of his inner temple, once completed, would be a very strong temple that could withstand any force in life.

This is an example of a spiritual dream. Sometimes you get these dreams, and you say, "What did that mean?" If it doesn't make any sense in a literal way, try to see what spiritual significance it has.

This building of his inner temple, once completed, would be a very strong temple that could withstand any force in life.

CATASTROPHE

A man who had just come into ECK had a spiritual dream. In this dream, he was standing in a room with some other ECK members. One of them said to him, "Did you drop that letter?" On the floor was an envelope.

He picked up the envelope. On the front was the address "Holy Child School," the name of a school he had attended as a child. In this dream "Holy Child School" meant the beautiful state of Soul.

The man wondered, *What does this envelope mean?* Then he saw something else: "Catastrophe" was also written on the envelope.

The dream was referring to his spiritual exercises. He hadn't been doing them. And this holy child, Soul, the spiritual being he is, was missing an opportunity to move ahead. He was creating, in fact, a catastrophe.

The dream was referring to his spiritual exercises. He hadn't been doing them.

This dream jolted him. "But what does it mean?" he asked. He wasn't quite sure, although he knew he hadn't been doing the spiritual exercises and he knew it was about the school he had attended, the Holy Child School.

So the next night, he had another dream. In this dream, he went back to the school and he saw that the whole place was in ruins. The walls used to be white; now they were all discolored by the weather and wear and tear of the years. He wanted to go upstairs to his former dormitory room, the place that had felt comfortable. He tried to climb the stairs, but his legs were too weak and he couldn't make it up. He crawled, finally, with great effort, and he was able to make it to the top of the stairs.

These two dreams came to the man right before an ECK seminar took place. And during the seminar, it came to him that he had been neglecting the Spiritual Exercises of ECK, the spiritual exercises that are in the discourses I write and that are available to members of ECK. So he began to do the spiritual exercises again.

SPIRITUAL EXERCISE RENOVATION

Half a year later, he had another dream where he went back to the Holy Child School. This time the place was being renovated. In other words, his inner bodies—the houses of Soul, the Emotional, Mental, and Causal bodies—were being restored building by building.

In the dream he wanted to go to the chapel. And this of course is the abode of Soul Itself, the realm of Soul on the Soul Plane.

When he went there, he saw the chapel had also been renovated, and its beauty was beyond description. It was so beautiful. Very beautiful, very white with the Light of God, which at Its very highest is pure white.

Colors of God's Light

Intermediate areas of God's Light are of all different colors, sometimes pink, orange, blue, or even green. Then It goes into the higher colors, colors of the intuition like purple and violet.

And then It moves into the first of the spiritual worlds. If you see a yellow light, it means you're now operating on the high spiritual planes. The yellow light moves to a faint yellow, and then It moves to a white, white light. You're into the higher areas of consciousness.

You're in your own worlds, the worlds of God. You have a right to be there. You should be there. And the Spiritual Exercises of ECK are the most direct way to get there. They are more effective than prayer.

Intermediate areas of God's Light are of all different colors, sometimes pink, orange, blue, or even green.

Listening to God

People misuse prayer by telling God what to do. Instead of listening to divine direction, instead of asking God, "What do you want me to do?" people misuse prayer.

Many times they thank God for the blessings they have in their lives. But too many times they say, "God, do this. God, do that." Makes you wonder about the Deity and patience. Where did the Deity get such patience? Probably from listening to prayers like that.

People misuse prayer by telling God what to do.

There's another step after listening to your dreams. There comes a time when you feel this need to share the teachings of ECK with others because this love inside you has grown.

It starts like a small burning heat of divine love, and it grows bigger and bigger inside your heart until it consumes you.

HEARTS FULL OF LOVE

But during this process where divine love comes in and takes over your heart, years may pass. It may be twenty years for some people. Others already have hearts full of love when they come into ECK.

These are the people who are always giving of themselves without asking for some kind of reward for what they've done. They're not asking for thanks. They just do what they do because they love God and they love people. And they do things that do not intrude into other people's space. In other words, you don't do for people what they don't want done for themselves.

One of the members of ECK was wondering how she could be an ECK neighbor.

One of the members of ECK was wondering how she could be an ECK neighbor. In other words, how could she tell other people about ECK or just be there listening to them in their hour of need.

Every day she asked, "What can I do today to be a vehicle for the Mahanta, the Living ECK Master? How can I be a good instrument for the Holy Spirit?" This was always on her mind.

In other words, she was asking, "How can I become a Co-worker with God?" This is what she wants to evolve into, spiritually.

One day, a couple were coming over to hang some new curtains for her. *How can I be available if they are interested in the ECK teachings, without pressing the teachings on them?* she wondered. Even though ours is a missionary teaching, a missionary path, it is a path that allows other people to have their freedom of belief and freedom of motion and movement. We don't push our teachings on people if they're happy with their own teachings.

We invite people to ECK events, and if they say, "No, thank you. I'm happy with what I have," that's good enough. We don't pester them day after day, week after week, so that when they see us coming, they hide. They're afraid to answer the phone.

And I think you know what I'm talking about because we've all been victims of that kind of proselytizing and that kind of missionary work because we opened the door to that sort of thing. Some people have a very good way of saying, "No, thank you. Thank you for inviting me, but I have a teaching of my own." And they smile very nicely, and that's it. There's no question.

But other people have trouble with this. It's as if they're not sure about their standing in their own religion or in ECK.

If they show any weakness when the missionary comes, they're in for an hour or two of listening to people who will not leave their living room. And there's just no way you can get them out. This is not what we do in Eckankar. That's not our way.

HANGING CURTAINS

The woman decided she could leave some dream brochures out on her bed because the people hanging the curtains would be coming into the bedroom. It was a husband-and-wife team.

When they came into the home, the husband went

k at the rooms where he was going to have to
oles to hang the curtain rods. "Let's go to your
m," the wife said to the ECKist, "and see what
kind of curtains we need there."

As they went into the bedroom, the wife saw the dream brochures on the bed. "Oh, dreams," she said. "I like dreams."

The ECK member said, "Dreams are important. Thousands of people around the world study dreams. They realize that this is God's way of speaking to them."

The woman said, "I've had this one dream for a long time. I go to this river, but it's getting late in the afternoon, and if it gets too much later, it's going to be dark. But I know I need to swim in that river." It was a very spiritual dream. But she didn't know what it meant. "What does this dream mean?" she asked the ECKist.

The ECKist said, "That's not for me to say." She gave some possibilities, saying it could mean this or that. But she said, "It's up to you to learn to interpret your own dreams."

The woman told the ECKist she had studied meditation in college and she had had some dreams where she had seen the future. Ever after, she had had this interest in dreams.

RIVER OF LIFE

The woman's dream was about the river of life. And the day was ending, night was drawing near, which meant that her time in the lower worlds was coming to an end. She was close to the time when she could bathe in this river of life, the current of God which we know as the Light and Sound.

With the spiritual exercises, you can bathe in this

...unds of people around the world study dreams. They realize that this is God's way of speaking to them.

With the spiritual exercises, you can bathe in this river, which is the river of divine love.

river, which is the river of divine love.

You can bathe in it, immerse yourself in it spiritually, and be purified. You can find the purification necessary to rise into higher states of consciousness, into spiritual freedom in this lifetime.

Talk Planning

As I plan a talk, I gather information for months ahead of time. But I don't put it together until the day of the talk. I used to try to do it a few days ahead of time, and I'd have the talk memorized but it was old news to me.

And if it was old news to me, it certainly would come across as old news to you. So I put myself on the cutting edge in giving these talks.

I have certain things I want to mention to you, but until about an hour or two before I actually put the talk together, I often have no idea what the title will be. No idea. So it's always exciting for me too.

At one seminar in St. Louis, just as I got to the seminar, my voice gave out. No voice. I was curious, how was I going to talk at an ECK seminar with no voice? And of course, that worked out too. My wife helped me on the first talk. And after that, I recovered enough of my voice to go through the rest of the seminar. That's how it is. We just keep moving ahead.

A Very Spiritual Journey

One woman was moving ahead—but very, very slowly. She and her husband lived on a farm in the U.S., and somehow they had won a trip to England and Scotland.

So they left the farm and went on their nine-day trip. As the couple was leaving for their trip, the woman told her husband, "I've been reading the Eckankar book *The Flute of God* for nine years. I feel this is a very spiritual trip; sometime during our vacation I'm going to get another book, take another step."

She was very cautious and careful about the path of ECK, about as cautious as a person can get. Many people wait a year or two or five to become a member of ECK. Nine years is really pushing it, especially when you have a young path such as ours. We've only been around since 1965 in recent times.

Their trip was very nice. They saw Scotland and England. But the last day of the trip came, and no great bright light of illumination had struck the woman, and she was disappointed.

She told her husband, "In forty-five minutes the cab is going to be here to take us to the airport, and I thought there was going to come this great spiritual insight to take me to the next step on my spiritual path."

He said, "Well, we could try to find a pastry shop. After all, if you can't get the spiritual food, you might as well go get some real food."

Europe is light years ahead of anyone else in the area of sweets. Mostly, these past years, I just look at dessert and use my imagination and my memory. My long memory from a past life and earlier in this life when I could eat anything and everything.

The couple walked around the block looking for a pastry shop, wanting one last treat before they went home. As they came around the corner, they saw a big sign on a building: ECKANKAR.

"Look," the wife said. "There's an Eckankar place here." It was very close to their hotel.

So they went in. A man was seated at a desk

Many people wait a year or two or five to become a member of ECK.

talking to another man who she felt looked just like a Hindu from India. The Americans were in a hurry. They said, "Look at all these ECK books." They were talking, wishing the Hindu man would hurry up, do his business, and leave so that they could talk to the man seated behind the desk. They wanted to ask a question, and the question was: I've read *The Flute of God* for nine years. It's been my bible. But I finally feel it's time for me to take the next step. What books do you recommend?

This is what they wanted to ask. But the Hindu man wouldn't go away.

THE FLUTE OF GOD

The woman and her husband began talking rather loudly. Talking about the ECK books, hoping their accent would give them away. Finally the man behind the desk got up and said, "Ah, I think I hear Americans." He went over to the husband, and the Hindu man came straight over to her. It was the strangest thing: she couldn't remember a thing he said to her, even while he was saying it, and he was speaking English.

He was an ECK Master in disguise, one of the many ECK Masters who help me in my mission here.

She put everything on the line right away, everything she wanted to say. She said, "I've been reading *The Flute of God* for nine years, but I now feel it's time for another step in my spiritual life. *The Flute of God* has been my bible. I have taken it everywhere with me. I have read it so many times."

This man looked at her as if she had a bug on her nose. He gave her a very hard stare, almost a critical stare. Basically, he was looking at her and saying, "Nine years! I can't believe it!"

He was an ECK Master in disguise, one of the many ECK Masters who help me in my mission here.

The Hindu man backed out of the front door and gave her one more hard stare. The woman was beside herself, she didn't know what to say. So she went over to the man from behind the desk.

"What were you talking about?" she asked him, because she figured it was the ECK center and they must have been talking about spiritual things.

"Well, we were talking about an ECK book," he said.

"Which one?" she asked.

"Just an ECK book," he said.

"No, no, which one? Which one?" she said, because she only knew one book and she wanted a recommendation for another step.

He said, "*The Flute of God.*"

And she said, "Well, then, what did you talk about?"

The man from behind the desk said, "That man had been reading *The Flute of God* for nine years, and he felt it was time to read something else."

The woman was beside herself. She said, "But that's my story!"

Finally the woman got a few ECK books, and now her trip to England was fulfilled. She knew it had been a spiritual trip. They left the ECK center just in time to catch their cab and make the flight back to America.

Sometimes the ECK, or Divine Spirit, works through me. And as It does, often even I am surprised.

She was just moving ahead, at the time rather slowly. But I guarantee if you stay in ECK, it will speed up.

AT THE POST OFFICE

Recently I was trying to help a young man move forward, but it really wasn't me. Sometimes the ECK, or Divine Spirit, works through me. And as It does, often even I am surprised. I'm out in the Soul body looking at this scene, watching myself in the physical body with someone else. And I say, "I can't believe I'm saying and doing that!" It's nothing outrageous, but it may be uncharacteristic.

It happened when my wife and I went to the post office to pick up our mail. She had to do some business there. It was going to take her another five minutes, so I said, "I'll wait by the car." I cleaned out our mailbox and walked out to the car.

It was a gorgeous day in Minnesota. The sun was shining. The sky was blue with just a few clouds. And there was a nice, light wind to move the mosquitoes along.

There is a chain with two firm posts to keep the general public from driving through an area where the post office trucks are parked. A boy was riding his bicycle through the parking area. He came up to this chain, which happened to be right by our car. He tried to squeeze by on his bicycle, but he didn't quite make it. He fell flat on the grass and on the curb.

He got up with a mild stream of private messages to God and gave his opinion about certain things. The boy was about eleven, I'd say, but he was good at heart. These were the things that you'd have to say to save face in front of a stranger. A little kid that age has got to save face, and he thought if you can rattle off some profanity, it makes you a man.

I asked, "Are you all right?" I was just being friendly. I knew he hadn't hurt himself. As soon as he got off the ground, he immediately went into his beggar spiel. He said, "Hey, mister, could you lend me a dollar? My buddy and I need . . ."

WORTH MORE THAN A DOLLAR

I couldn't believe it. He came at me with his hand out, and the next thing I knew, my finger was pointing in his face. I said, "Son, don't ever beg. You have a fine mind and body. You can be someone great." And then I put my hand down.

Suddenly I was looking at this scene from the viewpoint of Soul. I said to myself, "I can't believe I'm doing this." But it was with love and compassion that I was speaking with him. I didn't raise my voice, and I spoke with kindness, love, and concern, because I saw he was on the wrong path. He was cheating himself as a spiritual being. He wasn't using his creative powers of Soul correctly.

I said, "Son, don't ever beg. You have a fine mind and body. You can be someone great."

It must have been the force of Divine Spirit coming through me because after I said this, he stumbled backward as if some great hand had pushed him back. He fell on his bicycle which was lying on the ground. So for the second time, he was getting off the ground.

I leaned back against the car and looked at him. I remembered myself as a young person just about to become a teenager. The last thing you need then is a sermon. Because a sermon seals your eyes and ears shut. From that moment on, there's no communication with this world. There is no communication between the world of the child and the world of the adult.

He picked himself up fast, let me tell you. He just looked at me, and the last I saw of him, he was peddling furiously down the street. He never looked back.

When my wife got back to the car a few minutes later, I told her what had happened. And she said, "The Holy Spirit must have thought he was worth more than a dollar."

CRIMES AGAINST SOUL

Son and daughter, don't ever beg. I know we have the ECK Masters in disguise who come as beggars, but they're doing it to pass a blessing to the person they meet. And sometimes—who am I to say—it may be necessary to beg. But there are other ways to pay your own way in life. If you're needy, if you're on welfare or anything else that's necessary because of some condition you can do nothing about, that's fine. If you receive retirement or old-age benefits, you've earned them. You have earned the right to these benefits.

But there are so many people who are drawing benefits that they haven't earned. And they think they're getting something for free. Basically, they're professional beggars. And it's a crime against Soul.

If there's one crime—one spiritual crime—that you can do to yourself, it's to not use your God-given creative powers.

If there's one crime—one spiritual crime—that you can do to yourself, it's to not use your God-given creative powers. So use the resources around you and build a better place for yourself in this world. And you can't do it like a vulture. You can't do it like a crow living off the remains of others.

Just keep moving ahead.

HELP IN YOUR SEARCH FOR GOD

I feel like a news reporter in telling these stories. Some are my own stories. Most are yours. I'm just a reporter who reports on the spiritual news of today.

And so when I read *Stories to Help You See God in Your Life,* ECK Parables, Book 4, I said, "Yes, maybe the ECK, Divine Spirit, was using me to tell these stories. But they are your stories." And I told my wife, "We have some very good people editing and working on these stories, to put my talks into written form. They have done an excellent job."

I'd like to wish you well on your journey home and in your quest to find love. Because that is what this journey is all about.

But they're your stories; I'm just the reporter. These are stories of your experiences with the Holy Spirit, with the Light and Sound, with the miracles that have occurred in your life.

I knew the stories in the book. I had told them over the years. And yet I found them very interesting to read again. The stories come through clean and clear. I think they will help you in your own search for God.

I'd like to wish you well on your journey home and in your quest to find love. Because that is what this journey is all about.

ECK Summer Festival, Minneapolis, Minnesota,
Sunday, July 3, 1994

GLOSSARY

Words set in SMALL CAPS are defined elsewhere in this glossary.

ARAHATA. An experienced and qualified teacher for ECKANKAR classes.

CHELA. A spiritual student.

ECK. The Life Force, the Holy Spirit, or Audible Life Current which sustains all life.

ECKANKAR. Religion of the Light and Sound of God. Also known as the Ancient Science of SOUL TRAVEL. A truly spiritual religion for the individual in modern times, known as the secret path to God via dreams and SOUL TRAVEL. The teachings provide a framework for anyone to explore their own spiritual experiences. Established by Paul Twitchell, the modern-day founder, in 1965.

ECK MASTERS. Spiritual Masters who can assist and protect people in their spiritual studies and travels. The ECK Masters are from a long line of God-Realized SOULS who know the responsibility that goes with spiritual freedom.

HU. The most ancient, secret name for God. The singing of the word HU, pronounced like the word *hue,* is considered a love song to God. It is sung in the ECK Worship Service.

INITIATION. Earned by the ECK member through spiritual unfoldment and service to God. The initiation is a private ceremony in which the individual is linked to the Sound and Light of God.

LIVING ECK MASTER. The title of the spiritual leader of ECKANKAR. His duty is to lead SOULS back to God. The Living ECK Master can assist spiritual students physically as the Outer Master, in the dream state as the Dream Master, and in the spiritual worlds as the Inner Master. Sri Harold Klemp became the MAHANTA, the Living ECK Master in 1981.

MAHANTA.   A title to describe the highest state of God Consciousness on earth, often embodied in the LIVING ECK MASTER. He is the Living Word.

PLANES.   The levels of heaven, such as the Astral, Causal, Mental, Etheric, and Soul Planes.

SATSANG.   A class in which students of ECK study a monthly lesson from ECKANKAR.

THE SHARIYAT-KI-SUGMAD.   The sacred scriptures of ECKANKAR. The scriptures are comprised of twelve volumes in the spiritual worlds. The first two were transcribed from the inner PLANES by Paul Twitchell, modern-day founder of ECKANKAR.

SOUL.   The True Self. The inner, most sacred part of each person. Soul exists before birth and lives on after the death of the physical body. As a spark of God, Soul can see, know, and perceive all things. It is the creative center of Its own world.

SOUL TRAVEL.   The expansion of consciousness. The ability of SOUL to transcend the physical body and travel into the spiritual worlds of God. Soul Travel is taught only by the LIVING ECK MASTER. It helps people unfold spiritually and can provide proof of the existence of God and life after death.

SOUND AND LIGHT OF ECK.   The Holy Spirit. The two aspects through which God appears in the lower worlds. People can experience them by looking and listening within themselves and through SOUL TRAVEL.

SPIRITUAL EXERCISES OF ECK.   The daily practice of certain techniques to get us in touch with the Light and Sound of God.

SUGMAD.   A sacred name for God. Sugmad is neither masculine nor feminine; It is the source of all life.

WAH Z.   The spiritual name of Sri Harold Klemp. It means the Secret Doctrine. It is his name in the spiritual worlds.

INDEX

For Further Reading and Study*

Journey of Soul
Mahanta Transcripts, Book 1
Harold Klemp

This collection of talks by Eckankar's spiritual leader shows how to apply the unique Spiritual Exercises of ECK—dream exercises, visualizations, and Soul Travel methods—to unlock your natural abilities as Soul. Learn how to hear the little-known Sounds of God and follow Its Light for practical daily guidance and upliftment.

The Spiritual Exercises of ECK
Harold Klemp

This book is a staircase with 131 steps. It's a special staircase, because you don't have to climb all the steps to get to the top. Each step is a spiritual exercise, a way to help you explore your inner worlds. And what awaits you at the top? The doorway to spiritual freedom, self-mastery, wisdom, and love.

35 Golden Keys to Who You Are & Why You're Here
Linda C. Anderson

Discover thirty-five golden keys to mastering your spiritual destiny through the ancient teachings of Eckankar, Religion of the Light and Sound of God. The dramatic, true stories in this book equal anything found in the spiritual literature of today. Learn ways to immediately bring more love, peace, and purpose to your life.

How to Master Change in Your Life: Sixty-seven Ways to Handle Life's Toughest Moments
Mary Carroll Moore

In your life, you always have a choice. You can flee from change, a victim of *fate*. Or, as the hero, you can embrace each challenge you face with courage and grace. Included are sixty-seven powerful techniques to help you understand change, plan the future, conquer fear and worry, and resolve problems of the past.

*Available at your local bookstore.** If unavailable, call (612) 544-0066. Or write: ECKANKAR Books, P.O. Box 27300, Minneapolis, MN 55427 U.S.A.

There May Be an
Eckankar Study Group near You

Eckankar offers a variety of local and international activities for the spiritual seeker. With hundreds of study groups worldwide, Eckankar is near you! Many areas have Eckankar centers where you can browse through the books in a quiet, unpressured environment, talk with others who share an interest in this ancient teaching, and attend beginning discussion classes on how to gain the attributes of Soul: wisdom, power, love, and freedom.

Around the world, Eckankar study groups offer special one-day or weekend seminars on the basic teachings of Eckankar. Check your phone book under **ECKANKAR**, or call **(612) 544-0066** for membership information and the location of the Eckankar center or study group nearest you. Or write **ECKANKAR, Att: Information, P.O. Box 27300, Minneapolis, MN 55427 U.S.A.**

☐ Please send me information on the nearest Eckankar center or study group in my area.

☐ Please send me more information about membership in Eckankar, which includes a twelve-month spiritual study.

Please type or print clearly   940

Name _____
           first (given)   last (family)

Street_____ Apt. # _____

City _____ State/Prov. _____

ZIP/Postal Code _____ Country _____

About the Author

Sri Harold Klemp was born in Wisconsin and grew up on a small farm. He attended a two-room country schoolhouse before going to high school at a religious boarding school in Milwaukee, Wisconsin.

After preministerial college in Milwaukee and Fort Wayne, Indiana, he enlisted in the U.S. Air Force. There he trained as a language specialist at Indiana University and a radio intercept operator at Goodfellow AFB, Texas. Then followed a two-year stint in Japan where he first encountered Eckankar.

In October 1981, he became the spiritual leader of Eckankar, Religion of the Light and Sound of God. His full title is Sri Harold Klemp, the Mahanta, the Living ECK Master. As the Living ECK Master, Harold Klemp is responsible for the continued evolution of the Eckankar teachings.

His mission is to help people find their way back to God in this life. Harold Klemp travels to ECK seminars in North America, Europe, and the South Pacific. He has also visited Africa and many countries throughout the world, meeting with spiritual seekers and giving inspirational talks. There are many videocassettes and audiocassettes of his public talks available.

In his talks and writings, Harold Klemp's sense of humor and practical approach to spirituality have helped many people around the world find truth in their lives and greater inner freedom, wisdom, and love.

International Who's Who of Intellectuals,
Ninth Edition